The Whiddon Heritage

Hayes L. Whiddon, Jr.

authorHOUSE®

AuthorHouse™
1663 Liberty Drive
Bloomington, IN 47403
www.authorhouse.com
Phone: 833-262-8899

Published by AuthorHouse 10/19/2020

ISBN: 978-1-4389-2984-2 (sc)
ISBN: 978-1-4389-2985-9 (hc)
ISBN: 978-1-6655-0519-2 (e)

Library of Congress Control Number: 2008911610

Print information available on the last page.

This book is printed on acid-free paper.

To my beloved grandchildren,
Beau, Lacey, Jesse and Lilly.

One generation passeth away, and another generation
cometh: but the earth abideth for ever.
ECCLESIASTES 1:4

Contents

Part III
The Other Whiddon Lines of Descent

Line of Descent of John, Son of the Immigrant

Line of Descent of Augustine, Son of the Immigrant

Illustrations

Preface

After retirement in 1999, quite by accident, I became interested in the history of my family. As a frequent user of the internet I came across Edward Whiddon's web site, which provides the genealogy of the Whiddon family in great detail. His information dovetailed perfectly with research done by my daughter, Catharine, for a Girl Scout project. She put together data on our family going backward that met Edward Whiddon's information coming forward. This provided my family line back to its beginning in America. Almost at once this information fell into my hands and provided the spark that piqued my interest in Whiddon genealogy.

I had a coworker in the 1980s who was interested in genealogy and spent a great deal of time doing research on his family in Virginia. He told me that he often came across the Whiddon name in his research and wondered if I would be interested in joining him. At that time I had no interest in genealogy and doubted that this related to my family. I had always assumed that my family immigrated to Georgia from England because my family had lived in Decatur County, Georgia for more than a century before coming to Virginia in 1941.

However, I was to discover the beginning was here, where I live, in Chesapeake, Virginia. Chesapeake was incorporated as a city in 1963 from the area that was formally Norfolk County, where John the Immigrant landed in 1635. Geographic names that were familiar to the first Whiddons are commonplace in my world. I have children who attended both Western Branch High School and Deep Creek High School. At one time I owned a house on Paradise Creek. Four generations of my family worked at the Norfolk Naval Shipyard, located on the Southern Branch of the Elizabeth River. In fact, employment at the shipyard brought my father, grandfather, three uncles and their families to Norfolk County during the Second World War; they came with thousands of others to support the war effort. After the war my father was the only Whiddon to remain as the others returned to familiar surrounding in Georgia and Florida.

I believe the Whiddon story is interesting enough to warrant a book, one that will serve historical and personal purposes. The method I chose in writing this book was not to include as many historical record entries as possible but to tell about my family in narrative form. I have included records that I believe help tell the story. My goal was to make the story as human and personal as I possibly could. One of the great mysteries of genealogy is the why of a situation. The what, where and when can often be determined from available records but generally the why remains unknown.

Included in this book is a section on the Whiddons of Devon, a county of England. It is primarily concerned with the Whiddon family in the Chagford area of Devon.

I wrote an article on Captain Jacob Whiddon that was published in the journal of the Devon History Society. The article appeared in the fall 2007 issue of the Devon Historian, an expanded version is included in this book. The relationship of Captain Jacob Whiddon to the Whiddon family is undetermined.

I chose to research and write primarily about my direct line of descent; however, references to others that enhance the story are included. I tried to plow a straight, deep furrow instead of a broad, shallow coverage of the family as most have done. Beginning with John Whiddon, the Immigrant, I divide each generation into separate sections. The son who is in my direct line of descent is shown in bold typeface and is the subject of the following section.

Also, included are sections on the other two sons of the Immigrant. They are the interesting line of his oldest son John and the short line of Augustine.

The late Edward Whiddon was one of the Whiddon genealogists whose work and insights were extremely valuable in my research. He was a careful researcher whose work, as well as that of several others, was very helpful.

It has often been said by authors acknowledging someone who has benefited their work that it would not have been possible without that person; this has never been truer than in my case. My wife, Elaine, has been a constant encourager of my work and has been invaluable as my editor. She has kept me focused as a writer and ensured that the language in the book was uniform, clear and concise. She is also responsible for the artwork, including painting the Whiddon coat of arms. Most of the credit is hers.

My grandchildren provided the inspiration for me to research and write this book. They are my Whiddon legacy.

Part I

The Whiddons Of Tudor England

The Armorial Bearings of

WHIDDON

of Chagford in the County of Devon

The Whiddons of Chagford
in the County of Devon

Devon is a county in the southwest of England between the Bristol and English Channels. It is bound on the west by Cornwall and on the east by Somerset and Dorset Counties. The countryside is hilly with a huge granite plateau dominating the county. The highland is covered by broad moors with the largest being Dartmoor, it is considered southern England's most beautiful and rugged wilderness.

The area has a history of at least 4,000 years. Devon contains remains of Neolithic settlements and standing stones of druidic origin. During the Roman occupation it was dominated by the Celtic tribe of the Dumnonii, the Deep Valley Dwellers. Devon was a remote region with little Roman influence.

The ancient and small town of Chagford, located in Devon, was the home of the Whiddon family for several hundred years. The town was probably a hamlet in Saxon times. Its location was chosen for proximity to the river for water and to the hills for defense. Chagford is northeast of Dartmoor, in the Teign River Valley. The name Chagford is of Saxon origin, originally spelled Kageford and means the "gorsey" spot where the river is "forded". (Gorse is a shrub with fragrant yellow flowers that grows wild in Devon.) It is likely that the Teign Valley was cleared for farming by the Saxons. In 1086 the manor of Chagford was recorded in the *Domesday Book* as a farming community with sheep as the primary commodity.

Chagford Manor belonged to Sir Hugh Chagford in the reign of Henry III. It was sold in 1299 by Thomas de Chagford to Simon de Wibbery, who was rector of the church in 1315. His descendants held the manor for nearly two centuries until it passed into the hands of the Copelstones through intermarriage. It subsequently passed to the Whiddon family; which for generations was seated at Whiddon Park.

There is archaeological evidence of tin mining in the Teign Valley as early as Roman times. Chagford was made one of the stannary towns in 1305 by a charter granted by King Edward I. This established Chagford as an administrative center with authority to assay, stamp, tax and control the sale of tin. Also, established was a stannary court to administer laws concerning tin miners and tin-mining interest. This separate system of law and governmental administration reflects the importance of tin to the English economy during this period. At least 40% of Devon's tin production passed through Chagford in the 14th century. Chagford remained the dominant stannary town in Devon until the beginning of the 16th century.

In 1585 Sir Walter Raleigh was appointed by Queen Elizabeth as Lord Warden of the Stannaries. The tin industry brought tinners, merchants and king's officials to Chagford which greatly enhanced its economy. During the 16th century the Whiddon family was one of the largest owners of tin-mining land in the Stannary of Chagford.

The oldest surviving building in Chagford is the parish church. The church was dedicated to Saint Michael in 1261. The church as seen today dates from the 15th century and is a good example of a granite church of that period. The strong influence of tin mining in Chagford is evidenced by a boss, carved into the church's interior roof, of three rabbits joined together. This is the emblem of the local tin miners. The size and beauty of Chagford church is due in large measure to the wealth generated by tin mining. The churchyard includes many graves of members of the Whiddon family.

In 1530 the churchwardens of St. Michael's paid John Whiddon 7 shillings for legal work. He later became a judge of the King's Bench.

In the 1550s so many repairs were needed to the church that the parishioners borrowed one half-thousand weigh (600 lbs.) of white tin from John Whiddon. By 1560 the church obtained a new source of funds by purchasing the rights to the markets and fairs held in Chagford. These rights were purchased from John Whiddon, who owned the manor and advowson. Advowson was the right to appoint the parish priest.

At the end of the 15th century, Henry Tudor had become King Henry VII, Columbus had reached the New World, feudalism had ended and the English Renaissance had begun. The Tudor era was a time of intense and immense change in England. Along with other societal changes, Henry VIII brought about the English Reformation beginning in 1534. Devon, having been Catholic, became staunchly Protestant over the next few decades.

The feudal nobility lost influence in favor of merchants, freemen and yeoman farmers who became the new gentry. Merchants, seamen and lawyers gained in importance because of their greater value to the Crown based on changes in society and greatly increased exploration and trade. Lordship of the manor moved away from its feudal origins but continued as an indication of status. The lord of the manor still had great legal and financial clout and was considered one of the greater men of the day.

The woolen industry and overseas trade brought prosperity to all of England. In Devon the tin industry and busy seaports added to the economic well-being. Throughout this period Chagford remained a stannary town and was a thriving market town.

Devon was particularly well situated to take advantage of these changes. Her ports allowed the development of a great seafaring tradition. Much of the contact with other countries and the New World was through her ports. Also, many young men received good educations in the local schools and would then go on to Oxford or Cambridge or to the Inns of Court in London to receive training in the law. The developing society required a more sophisticated system of law and courts.

During this time of great change an old Devon family, residing in Chagford, begot Sir John Whiddon, Knight and Judge of the King's Bench. He made the Whiddon name one of national repute and accumulated great wealth for his family.

At the beginning of the 15th century the manor of Chagford was possessed by the Coplestones and the manor of Teigncombe was held by the Bonvilles. Chagford Manor was purchased by Sir John Whiddon in 1556 and Teigncombe came into possession of the Whiddon family during the reign of Elizabeth. The large manor of South Teign became the property of the Whiddon family under Sir John Whiddon. The manor Shapley was owned by the Prouz family from 1292 to 1639, when it came to the Whiddons.

The earliest record of a Whiddon dates from around the year 1300. His first name is unknown, as is that of his wife who was a daughter of the family de Chagford. He was probably a merchant or yeoman farmer of some status or he could not have married a daughter of the lord of the manor. Mr. Whiddon and Miss de Chagford surely prospered, as their son Henry married Jane Wray of London. This indicates contact with the capital suggesting that the Whiddons were merchants in the 14th century.

Henry and Jane, while residing in Chagford, had a son Richard. Richard and an unknown wife had a son named Simon, who married Margaret, daughter of Richard Wykes of Coketry in Devon.

Simon and Margaret were also residents of Chagford. Their son, John Whiddon of Chagford, married Joan Alford.

John Whiddon and Joan had a son also named John. The second John married a Miss Rugg. The Ruggs were an old Chagford family with numerous mentions in the records of the churchwardens. Both families were long established at Chagford.

It was the son of John and Miss Rugg who would greatly increase the family's fame and fortune. Born about the year 1500, John Whiddon was educated in Devon and then went to London to study law at the Inner Temple and would ultimately become a nationally renowned and respected jurist.

John was elected a reader in the autumn of 1528. His appointment as reader was renewed the following year and he was elected again in 1535. In 1538 he was chosen as treasurer of the Inner Temple and held the office for two years. John was nominated a serjeant-at-law by Henry VIII and, upon Henry's death, was confirmed by the new king, Edward VI. In 1553 immediately after Mary became queen, John was appointed a judge of the King's Bench and the following year was knighted. It was customary for judges of the King's Bench to receive the honor of knighthood. The King's Bench was held in Westminster Hall, with the king or queen usually presiding.

Until the reign of Queen Mary, judges rode mules to court. Mules were ridden as a sign of humility because, originally, all lawyers were ecclesiastics. Sir John Whiddon objected to this practice and with his refusal to continue it, the custom ceased. He was the first judge to ride to Westminster Hall on a horse instead of a mule.

In April 1557 Thomas Stafford led a rebellion and captured Scarborough Castle. The insurrection was put down by the Earl of

Westmoreland and the rebels taken prisoner. Judge John Whiddon was sent by Queen Mary to Yorkshire to conduct the trial of the prisoners. He was given the commission of general, providing him the authority to raise forces to quell any further rebellion. The situation was so dangerous that Judge Whiddon sat at the bench in armor. As a reward for his service the Queen gave Judge Whiddon an addition to his coat of arms. It was a golden-billed black swan sitting in a crown and the motto *Rara avis in terris, nigroque simillima Cygno,* meaning "a rare bird on earth and very like a black swan".

Judge Whiddon's appointment as judge of the King's Bench was reaffirmed by Queen Elizabeth when she assumed the throne. Judge Whiddon took part in the procession into the Chapel Royal when Elizabeth opened Parliament in 1563. He continued in this position the remainder of his life. He served as a serjeant-at-law for 46 years and as judge for 22 years.

Sir John Whiddon was married twice. His first wife was Anne Hollis, daughter of Sir John Hollis, Lord Mayor of London, with whom he had one daughter, Johanne. The second marriage was to Elizabeth Shilston, daughter and coheiress of William Shilston, Esquire. John and Elizabeth had six sons and seven daughters.

At the time of his death Sir John Whiddon was a substantial land holder with considerable tin mining interests. He owned the manors of Chagford and Teigncombe, leased the manor of North Bovey and leased other properties in South Tawton and Chagford. He also owned the Church House. The granite structure was originally built by the churchwardens in the early 16th century and was purchased by Sir John Whiddon in mid century. It served as a town house for the Whiddon family. After it passed out of the Whiddon family it became a tavern named the Black Swan Inn. Today, the restored mansion holds a significant place in Chagford as the Three Crowns Hotel.

Sir John Whiddon is buried in the chancel of St. Michael's Church in an imposing canopied alabaster chest tomb. It is the most impressive tomb to be seen in any of the high moorland churches. This splendid tomb bears the inscription, "Here lieth Sir John Whiddon, Kt., one of the Justices of the King's Bench, who ended this life the 27th January 1575". Sir John Whiddon's estate went to his six sons.

The oldest son, William, was admitted to the Inner Temple in 1553 to study the law. William was married twice, first to Mary Langdon and then Eleanor Basset. Neither marriage produced children. William died in 1573.

Edward, the second son, became the principle heir. He was admitted to the Inner Temple in 1559. Edward married Anna Chudleigh Coffin in 1568 and they had a son and heir named John. This John was knighted at the coronation of King James in 1603. He was lord of the manor of Chagford and a 1607 survey of the manor at South Teign showed him to be the largest landowner with 800 acres. At his death, he owned the manors of Shapley and Clifford Cully as well as land in 24 Devon and 5 Cornish parishes.

Sir John Whiddon, grandson of the judge, married Blanch Ashford and they had three sons. William was the oldest but he died before his father. A diminished inheritance went to the second son, Roger. Sir John Whiddon lost a number of properties as payment of debts. Both William and younger brother John died without having children. Roger had one daughter, Elizabeth, to whom he left his tin works of Tinmarsh, Smalebrook and Natbrooke and the tin works within the Stannaries of Chagford, Lydford, Tavistock, Plympton and Ashburton. His will shows that much of his property was given to others to pay off debts. The dwindling of family assets begun under Sir John Whiddon continued under son Roger. When Roger died in 1645 this branch of the family went into the female line.

Oliver, the third son of the judge, served as his father's executor. Oliver was admitted to Exeter College in 1563. He became an M.A. and a Fellow of the College. He became Rector of Yoxhall and Archdeacon of Totnes in 1568. At his father's death, Oliver received the family town house. It is located in Chagford, across from the St. Michael's Church. When Oliver died the family house passed to Francis, the fourth son.

Francis, the fourth son of the judge, was probably one of the men attempting to plant the first English colony in the New World. Sir Walter Raleigh received a charter to accomplish this and in 1585 sent a fleet of seven ships to the New World, among the mariners in this fleet was Jacob Whiddon. Many of the colonists were from Devon and among those recorded was 'Frauncis Whitton'. The following year found the 108 colonists who were left on Roanoke Island in dire circumstances because their supply ship failed to arrive. They returned to England when they were rescued by Sir Francis Drake. Francis married Margaret Carew and they had two sons, Oliver and Francis.

Oliver, the elder son of Francis, was a substantial land holder who lived at Woodhouse in Sidbury and owned land at Easton. Oliver married Margaret Crymes Coplestone. Their son Rowland married Frances Coplestone and became a Justice of the Peace in 1647 under Charles I and again in 1653 under the Commonwealth. Rowland inherited the lands of his father, including those at Easton. The family had lived at Easton, in Whiddon House, since the time of Judge Whiddon. It is located several miles from Chagford and the property includes a large deer park sitting on a gorge, descending to the Teign River. In 1649 Rowland extensively renovated Whiddon House. The family lost possession of the house and the deer park in the 17th century. The house stands today.

The story of Rowland's sister, Mary, is considered by many to be the basis for the novel *Lorna Doone*. In 1641 she was shot by a spurned lover on her wedding day. She is buried at St. Michael's Church where a stone slab was set into the church floor to memorialize her.

Francis the second married Anne Southmeade in 1622. In 1624 John Southmeade installed his Puritan son-in-law as rector of St. Andrew's Church in Moretonhampstead, Devon. Rev. Francis Whiddon remained there as rector through the years of the Civil War until his death in 1656. His book, *The Golden Topaz*, based on verse 14 of Hebrews chapter 13, was published in the year he died. St. Andrew's Church contains a memorial to Francis Whiddon, M.A. celebrating his 32 years as rector. Francis and Anne had a son also named Francis.

Francis the third studied for the ministry at Wadham College, Oxford and was ordained in 1657. In 1658 he became minister at Totnes but in 1662, after the return of the king, he was ousted from this position for nonconformity. After his dismissal, Francis continued to preach where and when he could. His meetings were constantly disturbed by the local authorities. On one occasion Francis and his hearers were indicted for riot because of his unauthorized preaching. He was successfully defended by his cousin Rowland Whiddon of Chagford, Esq. There was a strong Puritan leaning in the family.

Lawrence, the fifth son of the judge, married Alice, whose last name is unknown and was buried in North Bovey in 1616.

Nicholas was the youngest son of Judge Whiddon. He received a B.A. from the University of Oxford in 1572 and was rector of North Bovey until his death in 1593.

The Whiddons were the most powerful and influential family in Chagford during the Tudor Dynasty. The Whiddon family of the 16th and 17th centuries provided distinguished service to the church and the English legal system. They served well both God and country. The family declined in the 17th century and eventually disappeared from the area. The decline was due, at least in part, to their Puritan religious leanings and support for the Commonwealth.

Bibliography

Bellot, Hugh H. L. *The Inner and Middle Temple: Legal, Literary and Historic Associations*, Whitefish, MT: Kessinger Publishing, 2005.

Calamy, Edmund. *A Continuation of the Account of the Ministers, Lecturers, Masters and Fellows*, London: R. Ford, 1727.

Foss, Edward. *The Judges of England, from the Time of the Conquest*, London: Longman, Brown, Green, Longman & Roberts, 1857.

Hayter-Hames, Jane. *A History of Chagford*, London: Phillimore & Company LTD, 1981.

Russell, Percy. *The Good Town of Totnes*, Devonshire Association for the Advancement of Science, Literature and Art, 1964.

Sams, Conway Whittle. *The Conquest of Virginia, The First Attempt*, Norfolk, VA: Keyser-Doherty Printing Corporation, 1924.

Walcott, Mackenzie E. C. *The Memorials of Westminster*, Whitefish, MT: Kessinger Publishing, 2005.

Whiddons of Chagford, 1300 - 1650

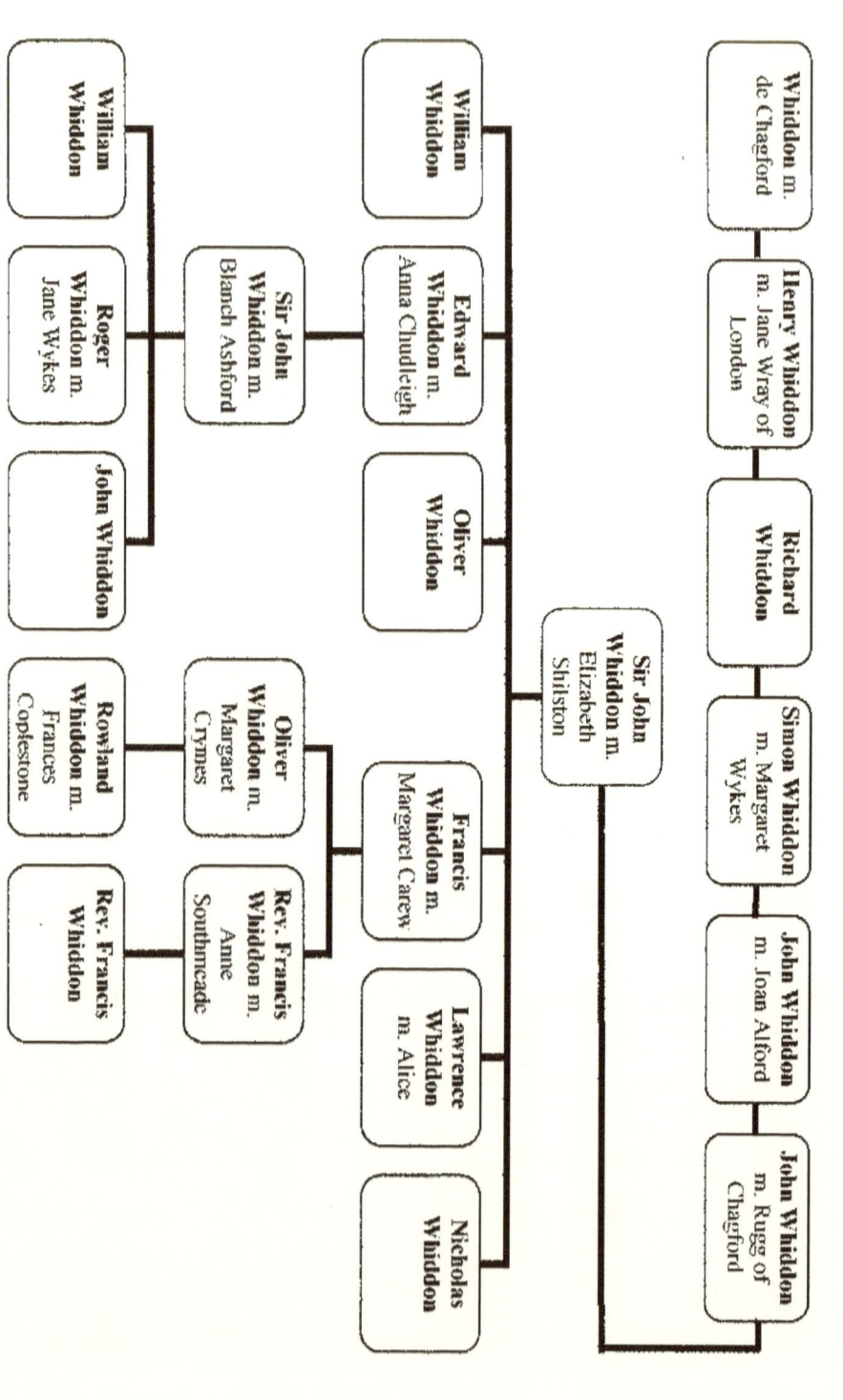

12

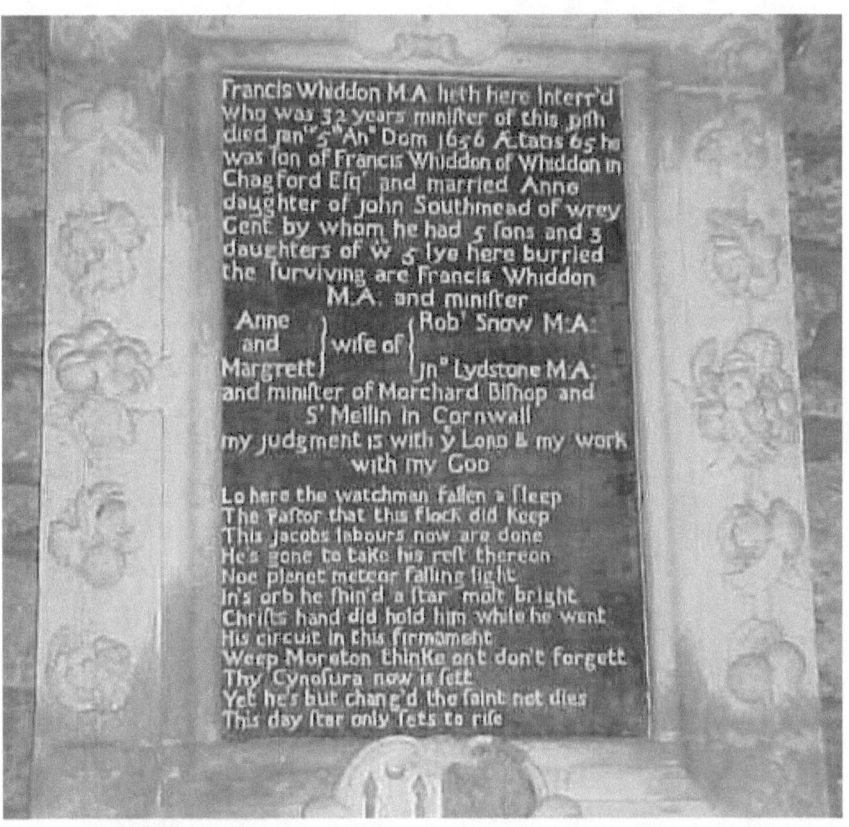

Whiddon Memorial in St. Andrew's Church, Moretonhampstead

St. Michael's Church and Three Crowns Hotel, Chagford

St. Michael's Church, interior view

Tomb of Sir John Whiddon in St. Michael's Church

Captain Jacob Whiddon

Jacob Whiddon was a new breed of mariner, adept in seamanship, naval tactics and trained in the latest science of navigation. He, like the great mariners of his time, was from the southwest of England, from the county of Devon. He was one of the intrepid Elizabethan seafarers, an extraordinary generation of seafaring men who won control of the oceans for England.

When Elizabeth took the English throne in 1558 she inherited a fleet of twenty-three ships. Elizabeth also inherited a solid administrative structure which she could use to strengthen the navy. Her father, Henry VIII, provided for the position of Lord Admiral and the Howard family had a near monopoly on the position for more than a century. In 1546 the Navy Board was founded to supervise the navy under the Lord Admiral. Henry also established three sites for the training of seamen, but Henry's lavish spending left England in tremendous debt. When Elizabeth wanted to increase English sea power she needed innovative ways to fund the navy.

English merchants were developing a new economic strategy, the joint-stock company, to finance ventures at sea. It was intended to fund voyages for discovery of the lands and riches of the New World. These companies were effectively used by Elizabeth to form a powerful royal navy. She issued letters of patent to authorize combination public-private ventures. Besides granting permission for a venture, she would usually provide some assistance in the form of ships, stores, gunpowder or money. The company would provide additional ships along with supplies and crew. This method reduced the financial strain on the royal treasury and provided Elizabeth with diplomatic cover against foreign protests.

These expeditions were not always used to explore new lands. The capture of foreign ships on the high seas often proved far more profitable than exploration. A captured ship with a valuable cargo yielded huge dividends. Well-established ratios for the division of the captured spoils existed, beginning with the Queen and going down through the company and the ship's captain and to the cabin boy. The English privateer came into existence because plunder on the high seas was more lucrative than exploration and colonization. Through these privateering activities England developed a generation of experienced sea captains and a good supply of seamen.

Sir Walter Raleigh understood the importance of sea power and wrote, "Whosoever commands the sea commands the trade; whosoever commands the trade of the world commands the riches of the world, and consequently the world itself".

Prior to this generation English sailors only sailed along the coasts or from island to island. Navigation on the open seas requires a different level of knowledge. Raleigh gathered experts in astronomy, geography and other sciences with nautical application. Among these experts was mathematician, philosopher and scholar, Thomas Hariot who provided scientific and professional instruction to Raleigh and his officers, including Jacob Whiddon. This resulted in new ways to navigate, new shipbuilding designs, better armaments and improved combat tactics. This occurred just in time because waiting on the horizon was a life-and-death struggle with Spain—a struggle that would determine control of the sea, the New World and the religious future of Europe.

The greatest English seafarers of this generation were all from Devon. This county in southwest England, on the peninsula that extends into the Atlantic, was the home of men like Walter Raleigh, Francis Drake, Richard Grenville, Humphrey Gilbert and the Hawkins family. Devon has the distinction of providing a large and brilliant group of naval commanders and daring seamen. These men took the lead in the conquest of Virginia and in breaking the power of Spain. In this company of mariners was Jacob Whiddon, an adept and courageous ship captain.

In the summer of 1578 Humphrey Gilbert received letters of patent for a substantial expedition of discovery and colonization. Although, this may have been cover for intended raids on Spanish interests in the Caribbean. Gilbert had a fleet of seven ships including the *Hope* of Greenway, with Carew Raleigh as captain and Jacob Whiddon as master. Also, part of Gilbert's fleet was the *Falcon* with Walter Raleigh as captain. The expedition was beset with many problems and ended when bad weather let them go no farther than Ireland.

On 30 January 1584 Sir George Carey, the governor of the Isle of Wight, wrote to Sir Francis Walsingham, the Secretary of State. Carey stated that he had received good information from Jacob Whiddon, master of a ship just returned from Lisbon, that Spanish preparations were underway to build a great navy that would carry thousands of soldiers to invade England. Whiddon had seen five galleons under construction and reported that one of them exceeded by half any previously built. King Phillip of Spain was determined to conquer England and depose Queen Elizabeth, as a service to God, because of the subversion of religion by the English. In the letter to Walsingham, Carey described Whiddon as a man "seeming to be sober, discrete and of reasonable judgment".

Walter Raleigh obtained a charter in 1584 from Elizabeth to establish a colony in any "heathen and barbarous lands" not inhabited by Christian people. In 1585 he sent a fleet of seven ships under the command of Richard Grenville that landed on Roanoke Island. Jacob Whiddon sailed with Richard Grenville to Roanoke and may have taken part in the abortive effort to relieve the colony in 1587.

In 1586 Raleigh sent two small ships, under the command of Captain Jacob Whiddon, on a privateering expedition. The *Serpent*, a bark of 35 tons, and *Mary Spark*, a bark of 50 tons, sailed out of Plymouth Harbor on 10 June to prey on shipping in the vicinity of the Azores. In due course, they encountered and captured a small ship containing, along with its cargo, the Portuguese governor of St. Michael's Island.

While they continued searching for Spanish shipping, the *Serpent* and *Mary Spark* displayed Spanish flags to disguise themselves as Spanish vessels. When they spotted a Spanish ship, they drew close, hoisted English flags and captured her. Onboard they found a Spaniard named Pedro Sarmiento, the governor of the Straits of Magellan. He was a valuable prisoner because he was a knowledgeable and experienced navigator, having sailed widely in the south Atlantic and Pacific Oceans. He possessed knowledge about parts of the world little known to the English.

While continuing to sail around the Azores they captured a third ship. It was laden with fish. Captain Whiddon let it go because he did not have sufficient hands to take it back to England. The following day they saw two Spanish vessels and chased them to Graciosa Island where the Spaniards came to anchor under the protection of a fort. Unable to get their ships close enough to the Spanish ships to board them, Whiddon decided to launch a small boat with nine men. Upon seeing the English row toward their ships the Spanish began to offload their men and as much cargo as possible to the shore. As the English continued to row toward the Spanish vessels, they drew fire from both the fort's cannon and small arms on the shore. When they reached the first vessel they cut her anchor cables, hoisted her sails and sent her off with two men. Then they rowed closer to shore to the second vessel, so close that the Spaniards on shore could throw rocks at them. They boarded this ship, cut her cables and hoisted her sails but she was so close to shore that she had to be towed to deeper water by the small boat. All the while they were under constant fire which they returned with the five muskets they had with them. They were able to take possession of the two ships without the loss of a single man.

The expedition resulted in five captured vessels with valuable cargoes and notable prisoners. Whiddon decided to release two of the vessels, as he did with the ship laden with fish. Also, released were all the Spanish and Portuguese prisoners with the exception of Pedro Sarmiento and three other important prisoners.

In early August, after their successful venture in the Azores, they set sail for England with the two captured ships and the important prisoners. On the way home they encountered a large Spanish fleet. They decided to engage, and in preparation sent the two captured ships ahead to England, leaving them with only 60 men in the *Serpent* and *Mary Spark*. The Spanish fleet consisted of 24 ships, including two great ships, one of 1,200 tons and the other of 1,000 tons. The remaining Spanish vessels consisted of 10 galleons and the rest were smaller ships filled with treasure, spices and sugars. The *Serpent* and *Mary Spark* attacked the Spanish fleet for 32 hours. The two large ships stayed between the Spanish fleet and the English. Unable to take any of the treasure ships and running out of gun powder, Whiddon was forced to break off the attack. The English were greatly disappointed at failing to enrich themselves with more Spanish treasure but happy they sustained no loss of men. The *Serpent* and *Mary Spark* fought the much superior force to a standstill.

They resumed their passage back to England and upon reaching Plymouth were joyfully hailed by the town, with cannons being fired. Using what little powder they had left, they returned the salute by firing their cannons.

Presently, they took the prizes and prisoners to Southampton to present them to Sir Walter Raleigh. Raleigh distributed shares of the prizes to Captain Whiddon and his men. Whiddon turned Pedro Sarmiento over to Sir Walter Raleigh who held him prisoner at Durham House, Raleigh's London residence.

Raleigh held Sarmiento in hope of a large ransom. Sarmiento was a special prisoner because he was an authority on the Incas as well as a highly experienced navigator. During his imprisonment at Durham House he filled Raleigh with tales of the fabled El Dorado, a land abounding with gold and laying in Guiana (Venezuela) between the Orinoco and Amazon Rivers. Raleigh was not to forget about El Dorado and its supposed riches.

In 1588 Spain assembled the largest fleet the world had ever seen. Phillip of Spain viewed the armada as a means of returning England to the Catholic realm. The Spanish fleet contained large ships intended to carry soldiers sufficient in number to board and capture enemy ships. The English had lighter, more maneuverable ships, designed as gun platforms intended to bombard the enemy with long-range cannon.

On 29 July 1588 Lord Howard was told that the 131ship Spanish Armada had been sighted off the Scilly Isles. Howard, Drake, Hawkins and Frobisher, each in command of a squadron, were caught in Plymouth Harbor and in danger of being bottled up and destroyed. Overnight, they escaped under cover of fog and when it lifted the Spanish realized that the English had the weather gauge and the advantage. The English were chasing from behind and with long-range shelling harassed the armada's progress. This used a tremendous amount of ammunition and supplies of ammunition were soon exhausted. Captain Jacob Whiddon, who was commanding Raleigh's *Roebuck,* was assigned to the squadron of Sir Francis Drake. Whiddon carried supplies of ammunition to the ships of the squadron and was employed in scouting duty.

On 31 July the Spanish fleet suffered two major disasters, including *Our Lady of the Rosary* accidentally colliding with another galleon and losing her bowsprit and foremast. She was left adrift. At dawn the following morning the crippled *Rosary* found herself only three cable lengths from Drake's *Revenge* and Whiddon's *Roebuck.* The *Rosary,* the richest prize captured in the entire campaign, soon capitulated. She yielded forty-six guns, other arms, ammunition and 55,000 ducats of gold. Drake transferred the gold to the *Revenge* before the *Roebuck* towed the *Rosary* into Torbay. Coffers containing "clothes of gold and other furniture" were found on the *Rosary* and were appropriated by the *Roebuck's* crew. Whiddon removed ten brass cannons and some tons of gunpowder from the *Rosary* to resupply the English fleet.

The Spanish were ultimately defeated by the more maneuverable English ships which pursued and harried them up the channel. The English by using long-range tactics and with help from the Dutch totally frustrated the Spanish. The armada was unable to accomplish its objective of escorting troops across the channel to a landing in England. With the English guns behind them, they chose to escape by sailing up the east coast of England and around Scotland and Ireland. On 12 August Lord Howard called off the chase. On the return to Spain the armada encountered a very severe storm off the Scottish coast that caused losses more devastating than the campaign against Lord Howard's fleet. The armada finally limped into Spanish ports having incurred losses of more than 15,000 men and almost 60 ships.

After the defeat of the Armada the Spanish navy was in a very weak position. The English privateers had free rein and more than 90 ships were captured and brought to England in a year. This was the largest haul of Spanish vessels ever made and Raleigh's ships brought in their share. Captain Jacob Whiddon was a trusted captain of Raleigh's privateering fleet and in 1590, commanding the *Pilgrim*, he captured, among others, a valuable Brazilian prize. A Dutch source stated that the English "are become lords and masters of the sea and need fear no man".

The success of the English privateers caused King Phillip of Spain to delay shipment of silver from the West Indies for fear of its capture. Phillip determined that the silver would not sail for Spain until he had sufficiently rebuilt his fleet to be able to protect it. Immediately after the disastrous lost of ships the armada suffered in 1588, Spain began a major shipbuilding program, including twelve enormous vessels called the Twelve Apostles.

The English, knowing Spain could not indefinitely hold the shipments, devised a plan to catch them. Ships would be positioned between the Azores and Spain to lie in wait. In early 1591 the English sent a squadron under the command of Lord Thomas Howard for this purpose. The squadron included Sir Richard Grenville on the *Revenge* and Captain Whiddon on the *Pilgrim*.

Lord Howard's squadron was at sea for six months and because of the inevitable filth of a long stay at sea sickness struck the crew in the form of typhus. It was absolutely necessary to find a port to replace the filthy ballast with clean rocks and to obtain fresh water and clean air for the sick. They put in at Flores in the Azores and carried the sick ashore to recuperate. Spain became aware of the English presence and sent a fleet of 53 ships to confront them. Howard received word of the approaching Spanish fleet from an English merchant. There was barely time to bring the sick aboard and depart the harbor before the Spanish fleet arrived. All escaped except Grenville on the *Revenge*. He was caught between two Spanish squadrons.

When the *Revenge* finally made sail an opportunity to escape presented itself. However, Grenville refused to run, not willing to dishonor himself, his country or Her Majesty's ship. A narrow gap between the Spanish squadrons gave him the idea to sail through it, firing his cannons, both port and starboard, to drive the Spanish apart so he could sail through and rejoin Howard. As Grenville sailed into the midst of the Spanish fleet the wind worked against the *Revenge* and she lost her advantage of speed and maneuverability.

The captain of the giant *San Philip*, one of the Twelve Apostles, sailed at the *Revenge* and when she was on top of the *Revenge* her huge sails blocked all the wind, leaving the *Revenge* becalmed in the middle of the Spanish fleet. Howard's fleet offered what little help it could. As the day wore on Grenville's situation grew worse and "none appeared in sight but enemies, saving one small ship called the *Pilgrim*, commanded by Jacob Whiddon, who hovered all night to see the success. But in the morning bearing with the *Revenge*, she was hunted like a hare amongst many ravenous hounds, but escaped". Captain Whiddon gallantly risked all to support Grenville, with whom he had earlier sailed to Roanoke.

The *Revenge* was surrounded by the enemy and had no hope of escape. First the *San Philip* and then the *San Barnabe* grappled and attempted to board. The *Revenge* repelled these attempts. As many as fifteen ships came against the *Revenge* to board her and all were beaten off. The *Revenge*, now barely afloat, was still taking a heavy toll on the enemy.

The Spanish ships carried musketeers who poured a steady barrage onto the decks of the *Revenge*. Grenville was hit several times by musket shot and eventually succumbed to his wounds after being transferred to the Spanish flagship. The *Revenge* negotiated favorable terms of surrender before ending the battle. The Spanish admired gallantry and certainly respected the heroic fight of the *Revenge* and its commander, Grenville, who displayed such valor.

Alfred Lord Tennyson's poem *The Revenge—A Ballard of the Fleet* describes this saga, considered to be greatest in English naval history. This battle was made famous by Raleigh's account which was based on eyewitness reports. This is a story about the courage and boldness of Devon mariners and Jacob Whiddon was a heroic player in this drama.

The interest that the captured Spaniard Sarmiento sparked in Raleigh in 1586 about the legendary El Dorado remained vivid. In 1594 Raleigh was ready to act. From his privateering captains he chose Jacob Whiddon, the man who had captured Sarmiento, to launch a reconnaissance voyage to Guiana. If an English foothold could be established in Guiana a wedge would be driven between the Spanish colonies of Mexico and Peru and the flow of gold to Spain would be cut off. This it was believed would topple the Spanish empire and provide enormous wealth to England.

Arriving at Trinidad Whiddon obtained permission from Don Antonio de Berrio, Spanish governor of Guiana, to resupply his ship. While supplies were being loaded Whiddon had a cordial meeting with Berrio, making discrete inquires about Guiana. Whiddon also met with the Indians for trade and to find out what they could tell him about El Dorado. Whiddon met an Indian Chief named Cantyman, whom he would see again on the return trip. When Whiddon was away from his ship Berrio sent some Indians to offer a deer hunt to the crew. Eight of them went ashore for the hunt and were attacked and killed by Berrio's men. Berrio had given his word to Whiddon that the English could "take water and wood safely"; this Spanish betrayal would not be forgotten. Whiddon knew it was time to leave and immediately sailed for England with information gathered from the Spanish and the Indians concerning the location of El Dorado. He brought back with him four Indians to be trained as interpreters and to provide details concerning area geography. These four comprised the largest group of Americans to have visited England to this point and provided valuable service to Raleigh on the return trip to Guiana.

Later, Whiddon was arrested based on charges brought by Dutch merchants. To free him and have him available for a return to Guiana, Raleigh had his political ally, Sir Robert Cecil, write to the judge of the Admiralty Court asking for his prompt release. Cecil wrote, "I pray Sir take some paines in the matter, and let it be so carried as Whydden may be forthwith at lybertie, for I assure yow, it concernes Sir Walter very nere, and yow shall therby doe such a curtesie to me and him as wee shall both thincke our selves beholdinge unto yow". This worked and Whiddon was available for a return voyage to Guiana to discover El Dorado.

Prior to the voyage to Guiana Thomas Hariot was consulted to provide the latest advances in navigation. He delivered a series of lectures to the captains and masters of the Guiana fleet. The lectures covered the latest research on navigational techniques. The cross-staff, an instrument held to the eye and used to determine latitude, always gave trouble because of facial differences. Mariners usually made a rule-of-thumb correction to the associated mathematical tables. Hariot developed corrected tables for Raleigh, Whiddon and shipmaster John Douglas based on their facial characteristics. They were prepared with the latest navigation techniques.

On 6 February 1595 three ships making the Guiana voyage sailed out of Plymouth Harbor. The ships were packed with soldiers and prospectors. The expedition was led by Raleigh who sailed on his flagship *Bark Raleigh*, commanded by Captain Whiddon. Whiddon was the old salt of this voyage. Sailing with the *Bark Raleigh* was a Spanish gallego, which was previously captured by a privateer, and a small bark. The *Lion's Whelp* was to sail with them but was delayed several days. Off the coast of Portugal, one of the three ships, the gallego, was blown off course and separated from the others. Upon reaching the Canary Islands on 17 February the two ships put in to rest and wait for the *Lion's Whelp* and the gallego. After waiting about a week and seeing no sign of the missing ships Raleigh decided to continue the journey.

The *Bark Raleigh* and the small bark arrived at Trinidad on 22 March. They anchored off Icacos Point, encountering neither Spanish nor Indian. After a few days for recuperation and reconnaissance they began to move north and on 4 April were off Port of Spain. Here they saw a small company of Spaniards guarding the landing. Raleigh sent Captain Whiddon to speak with them because he spoke Spanish. After a friendly meeting some of them came aboard. Later that evening the Indian Chief Cantyman, whom Whiddon had met on his 1594 voyage, came on board. From Cantyman they learned the strength of the Spanish garrison and its location in San Jose, the capital of Trinidad.

Over the next few days the Spanish guards came aboard the *Bark Raleigh* to trade and while on board they were wined and dined. Gaining the confidence of the Spanish, the English discreetly inquired about Guiana and navigation on the Orinoco River. Then on the evening of 7 April Raleigh decided to attack San Jose. They set upon the Spanish guards "putting them to the sword". They then marched about 100 men toward San Jose for a dawn raid. At sunrise they attacked and the Spanish were either killed or fled and Raleigh had taken the town and captured Berrio. Berrio was the one who killed eight of Whiddon's men during the 1594 visit. They looted and razed the town and after two days returned to the harbor with the captured Berrio. The same day the *Lion's Whelp* and the gallego came into view. April 10 was a good day for the English; they gained revenge for the killing of Whiddon's men, sacked the Spanish garrison, captured Berrio, established good relations with the Indians and were rejoined by their missing ships.

About 13 April they left Port of Spain and headed south, back to Icacos Point. There they built a wooded fort to serve as a base from which to explore the mainland and as a garrison against the Spanish. This put them only 10 miles from the South American coast. At this point the interrogation of Berrio was conducted to learn all that he knew about Guiana. From this base, Whiddon made a trip across the gulf to the mainland and discovered a suitable place to enter for the trip up the Orinoco.

Whiddon accompanied Raleigh and about 100 men as they crossed over to the South American mainland on 17 May. They crossed in five small boats because the Orinoco River delta was so shallow that larger vessels could not enter. It took fifteen days to traverse the delta, struggling against a strong current, extreme heat and shortages of food and water. Once through the delta and into the main river progress was much easier and faster. Five more days' travel on the river brought the party to the confluence of the Orinoco and Caroni Rivers, nearly 250 miles from their ships. Further passage upriver was impossible because of the falls ahead; therefore, three scouting parties were sent out on foot to explore the area. One of these scouting parties was led by Jacob Whiddon with the mission of finding signs of gold and "mineral stone".

It was nearly four weeks since they started the journey up the Orinoco. Encountering insurmountable obstacles of the falls, raging rapids, imminent rains and an exhausted crew they decided to end the Orinoco exploration. The swift current carried them downriver and in four or five days they were back at their base on Trinidad. Raleigh resolved to return the following year, but it was not to be.

Shortly after arriving at their base Raleigh's small fleet of ships sailed to Margarita and then to Cumana, a small town on the mainland. Cumana was a trading port for gold and tobacco and was often visited by English mariners. On 23 June the fleet launched five boats loaded with 210 men to loot and burn the town. Upon landing they quickly captured the waterfront and soon took control of the high ground. The Spanish regrouped at their fort and when reinforcements arrived they counterattacked. The town was better defended than Raleigh expected; casualties begin to mount and the English retreated to the shore. With great loss of life and many wounded they returned to their vessels.

Forty-eight were left dead on the shore, and another twenty-seven died of their wounds onboard ship. There was a total seventy-five dead, including Captain Whiddon. He was buried on Trinidad. The loss of Whiddon touched Sir Walter Raleigh who wrote concerning his faithful friend, "a man most honest and valiant, whom to my great sorrow I left buried in the sands of that island".

Captain Jacob Whiddon had a daughter and three sons christened at St. Andrew's Church in Plymouth: Annis in 1583, Jacob in 1584, Richard in 1587 and Halse in 1588. Jacob may have married a Halse, with that being the origin of the name of the youngest son.

The 19th century cleric and writer Charles Kingley describes Jacob as "a Devonshire man—probably one of The Whiddons of beautiful Chagford". J. T. White, in his *The History of Torbay*, describes Captain Jacob Whiddon as "a commander as daring as any in the fleet".

Jacob Whiddon was a stalwart 16th century seadog. He and his contemporaries laid the foundation that provided England the largest and most powerful navy in the world. "Britannia rules the waves" was a true statement for more than 300 years.

Bibliography

Adamson, J. H. & Folland, H. F. *The Shepard of the Ocean*, Boston: Gambit Incorporated, 1969.

Andrews, Kenneth R. *Trade, Plunder and Settlement*, New York: Cambridge University Press, 1984.

Kingsley, Charles. *Sir Walter Raleigh and His Time*, Project Gutenberg Ebook, 2002.

Mattingly, Garrett. *The Armada*, New York: Houghton Mifflin Company, 1987.

McDermott, James. *England and the Spanish Armada: The Necessary Quarrel*, Yale University Press, 2005.

Miller, Helen Hill. *Captains from Devon*, Chapel Hill, NC: Algonquin Books, 1985.

Nicholl, Charles. *The Creature in the Map*, University of Chicago Press, 1995.

Noble, T. C. *The Names of Those Persons Who Subscribed Towards the Defence of this Country at the Time of the Spanish Armada, 1588*, London: Alfred Russell Smith, 1886.

Raleigh, Sir Walter. *The Discovery of Guiana*, Project Gutenberg Ebook, 2006.

Trevelyan, Raleigh. *Sir Walter Raleigh*, New York: Henry Holt and Company, 2002.

Devon, Glorious Devon

Written by Sir Harold Boulton

Combe and tor, green meadow and lane,
birds on the waving bough.
Beetling cliffs by the surging main,
rich red loam for the plough.
Devon's the font of the finest blood
that braces England's breed.
Her maidens fair as the apple bud
and her men are men indeed.
When Adam and Eve were disposed
of the garden, hard by Heaven,
they planted another one down in the west -
t'was Devon, t'was Devon, glorious Devon.
Spirits to old world heroes wake
by river and cove and hoe.
Grenville, Hawkins, Raleigh, Drake
and a thousand more we know.
To every land the wide world oer
some slips of the old stock roam.
Leal friends in peace, dread foe in war,
with hearts still true to home.
Old England's counties, by the sea,
from East to West are seven,
but the gem to that fair galaxy
'tis Devon, 'tis Devon, glorious Devon.
Dorset, Somerset, Corn'all, Wales
may envy the likes of we.
For the flower of the West, the first, the best,
the pick o' the bunch us be.
Squab pie, junket and cider brew,
richest of cream from the cow.
What'd old England without 'em do,
and where'd un be to now?
As crumpy as a lump of lead
be a loaf without good leaven,
but the yeast Mother England did use for her bread
be Devon, be Devon, glorious Devon.

Part II

My Line Of Descent

Virginia in 1635

As early as 1498 John Cabot sailed along the eastern seaboard of North America. John Hawkins made his first trip to the New World in 1562. Other Englishmen, including Sir Francis Drake and Sir Martin Frobisher, made voyages across the Atlantic. Between 1585 and 1589 Sir Walter Raleigh made two unsuccessful attempts to establish a colony on Roanoke Island.

At the beginning of the 17th century England was still without a valid claim to any part of the New World. In 1606 James I chartered two companies, the London Company and the Plymouth Company, to establish colonies in North America. The London Company was first to embark, on 20 December of that year, when Admiral Christopher Newport departed London with the *Susan Constant, Godspeed* and *Discovery*. They were provided three objectives: find gold, find a passage to the Orient and find the Lost Colony of Roanoke. Adverse winds held the three ships near England for six weeks and seriously depleted their food supplies. Forty-five died on the voyage but 101 men and 4 boys finally touched land in Virginia on 26 April 1607. On 13 May they landed on a semi-island in the James River and established the first permanent English colony in the New World; they called it Jamestown.

When they sailed into Chesapeake Bay and up the James River they saw what looked like paradise for Virginia is beautiful in May: the deep forests of green, wild flowers in bloom, wide rivers full of fish, woods full of game and the sky filled with birds. Captain John Smith wrote of Virginia, "heaven and earth never agreed better to frame a place for man's habitation".

However, what they found was a formidable land filled with Indians and hard work. The mortality rate was high. Up to 40% of new arrivals died in their first couple of years. Malaria and intestinal disorders either killed or left survivors in poor health and prey to other diseases. In the early years of the colony starvation was a major cause of death. By the end of the first year in Jamestown only 38 of the original 105 colonists remained.

In 1614 the first shipment of tobacco went from Virginia to London; this proved to be a truly momentous event. Tobacco became very popular in Europe and brought prosperity to the growers and enormous import duties to the royal treasury. Tobacco turned the failure of the Virginia colony into a great success. The settlers had not found gold or a passage to the East but they found tobacco and it ensured Virginia would be a permanent English colony. Failure to find treasure, like Spain found in South and Central America, led most of the soldier-adventures to leave the colony; they would not hang up their swords to take up the hoe. Tobacco created the need for land along the waterways of Virginia and for abundant cheap labor. The entire area became known as the "Tobacco Coast".

The need for labor to work the tobacco fields was filled through immigration. Immigration into Virginia was so great that the population grew rapidly. From the 105 men and boys who settled Jamestown in 1607 the population grew to 900 in 1620 and 6,000 in 1635. The peak period for immigration was between 1630 and 1660 but the growth of tobacco farming caused a constant need for cheap labor throughout the entire 17th century. Because of high mortality rates and low birth rates, due to a lack of women for marriage, Virginia was basically an immigrant society until the end of the century. The colony depended on a constant influx of new arrivals from English provinces to sustain the population and allow economic growth. Without this large scale immigration the colony would have failed.

The principle cause of migration out of England was the large growth of the population which had risen by 40% from 1580 to 1640. This placed a strain on rents and food prices and along with the collapse of the textile industry caused widespread poverty. Large numbers of poor tramped England looking for work; many young men moved to London to find employment and finding none were ready to cross the Atlantic to make their fortunes.

Emigrants were either those who paid for their own passage or those who could not pay the fare and went as indentured servants. They bound themselves for a term of three to five years in return for their passage. Throughout the 17th century indentured servants outnumbered free emigrants by three or four to one. Both groups were predominantly young, male and single. For every woman who departed London for Virginia in 1635, six men emigrated.

As land became more sought after for the growing of tobacco, settlement expanded around Jamestown, then south across the James River and finally in the late 1620s into what would become Lower Norfolk County. Settlement of Lower Norfolk County lagged about a decade behind other areas south of the James River. Movement into Lower Norfolk County in the 1630s was due to increased immigration with the return to the system of granting headright patents.

Headrights were the dominant form of Virginia grants until 1699. Their origin was in the Greate Charter of 1618: "That for all persons... which...shall go into Virginia with the intent there to inhabite. If they continue there three years or dye after they are shipped there shall be a grant made of fifty acres for every person...which grants shall be made respectively to such persons... at whose charges the said persons going to inhabite in Virginia shall be transported...".

In the 17th century the common method of obtaining land was the headright system. The system was designed to encourage emigration. As stated in the charter, the headright provided the right to fifty acres of land for each person transported into Virginia. Headrights were claimed by the person who paid the passage for the emigrant.

The process of obtaining a patent for the land under the headright system included petitioning the county court for a certificate of importation. This petition included the names of those imported. The certificate was then taken to the Secretary of the Colony who issued a right to fifty acres for those listed on the certificate of importation. This right was then taken to the county surveyor who drew a plat for the chosen acreage. All these papers were then returned to the Secretary and a patent was issued.

Once the patent was issued two conditions must have been met to secure the property. First, a Quit Rent or annual payment to the Crown of one shilling per fifty acres must be paid. Second, either a house must be built and livestock kept or at least one acre must have been under cultivation within three years.

Because there was not a way to validate headright usage, headrights were often claimed more than once. Clerks either did not identify or ignored duplicate rights, so the same certificate of importation might be used more than once or the same person listed on multiple certificates.

By the year 1635 few believed that Virginia offered easy riches but many saw a chance, through hard work, to obtain land and a better life than was available to them in England. This was the world that John Whiddon entered to start our family's American journey. He must have been a young man of great courage to cross the Atlantic and step into the New World.

Bibliography

Games, Alison. *Migration and the Origins of the English Atlantic World,* Cambridge: Harvard University Press, 2001.

Horn, James. *Adapting to a New World: English Society in the Seventeenth-Century Chesapeake,* Chapel Hill: University of North Carolina Press, 1994.

Smith, Lacey Baldwin. *This Realm of England 1399 to 1688,* Lexington, KY: D.C. Heath and Company, 1976.

American Generations

NAME/WIFE	BIRTH DATE/PLACE	DEATH DATE/ PLACE
John Whiddon unknown	1619/ England	Unknown/ Lower Norfolk Co., VA
William Whiddon Ann Smith	1660/ Lower Norfolk Co., VA	1720/ Norfolk Co., VA
William Whiddon Dinah	1700/ Norfolk Co., VA	1780/ Nash Co., NC
William Whiddon, R. S. Mary Eason	1755/ Edgecombe Co., NC 1760/	1818/ Emanuel Co., GA 183?/ Emanuel Co., GA
Eli Whiddon Dicy	1780/ Nash Co., NC 1780/	1834/ Decatur Co., GA 1843/ Decatur Co., GA
David Whiddon Dicey Hayes	1828/ Decatur Co., GA 1828/ Jasper Co., GA	1858/ Decatur Co., GA 1862/ Jackson Co., FL
Henry William Whiddon Letitia Martin	26 Oct 1856/ Decatur Co., GA 31 May 1865/ Liberty Co., GA	22 Sep 1922/- Decatur Co., GA 30 Sep 1942/ Gadsden Co., FL
Jesse David Whiddon Amanda Earnest	6 Jan 1891/ Decatur Co., GA 7 Sep 1895/ Decatur Co., GA	15 Apr 1960/ Gadsden Co., FL 15 Feb 1977/ Madison Co., AL
Hayes Louis Whiddon Wyolene Philmon	25 Aug 1918/ Decatur Co., GA 12 Feb 1920/ Houston Co., GA	

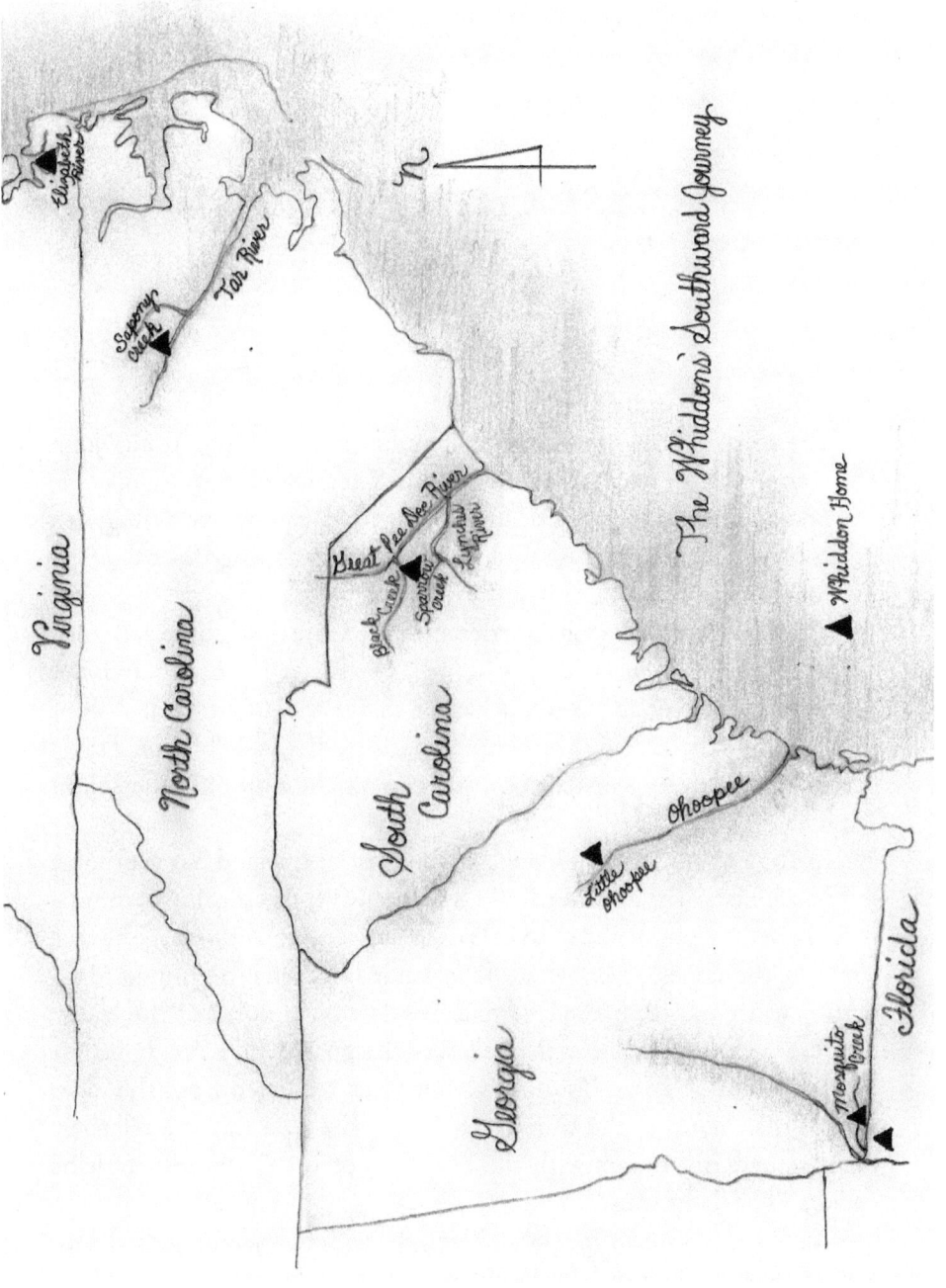

The Whiddons' Southward Journey

First Generation
John Whiddon, the Immigrant

The ship *Transport* sailed from London in July 1635. Young John Whiddon was a passenger onboard when it arrived in Virginia. He embarked either in London or in Plymouth, Devon, where ships often called before making the Atlantic crossing. He was listed as passenger Witton, Jo, age 16.

The *Transport* arrived in America and sailed into the Southern Branch of the Elizabeth River, a tributary of the James River. The Elizabeth River provided a sheltered, deep-water harbor that could accommodate ships from around the world. The American story of the Whiddon family began when sixteen-year-old John stepped off the ship onto the soil of Virginia.

In 1635 Virginia was no longer an outpost of England but was home to the colonists. The area north of the James River was already becoming prosperous and populated with at least twenty large plantations. The area south of the James River, where John landed, was just beginning to fill with new arrivals from England and overflow from north of the James. The area where John disembarked was designated in 1637 as Lower Norfolk County. Lower Norfolk County was separated from the older part of the colony by the wide James River. The land was still relatively desolate and encounters with the remnants of the Chesapean Indians could still be dangerous.

About this same time John Yates, a shipwright, immigrated into Lower Norfolk County. John Whiddon may have apprenticed with Yates to learn the trade of shipwright. Yates had a son, Richard, who was about Whiddon's age. Richard's daughter Joan married John Whiddon's oldest son, John. This apprenticeship with John Yates began what was to become a long and prosperous association with shipbuilding and trade for John Whiddon's oldest son and his descendents.

John's connection with his English forebears has not been determined but it is probable that he is one of the Whiddons of Devon.

John Whiddon was born about 1619 in England. The date of his death, in Lower Norfolk County, is not known. The name of his wife or wives is unknown.

John had the following children:

Name	Born	Spouse
John Whiddon	ca. 1644	Joan Yates
William Whiddon	ca. 1660	Ann Smith
Augustine Whiddon	ca. 1662	Sarah Cherry

Second Generation
William Whiddon

William, the second son of the Immigrant, was born about 1660 in Lower Norfolk County. William and his brother Augustine appear to be considerably younger than their brother John. They may be the sons of a second marriage of their father.

William's first appearance in the historical record was in 1678 on the certificate of importation of his brother John. Based on this certificate John was granted 300 acres.

William married Ann Smith, the daughter of Jacob and Elizabeth Smith, about 1687. Jacob Smith originally emigrated into Charles City County, an older part of the colony north of the James River. Later, Smith moved south into the less densely populated Lower Norfolk County where he received a grant for 300 acres in 1663. William purchased 50 acres from him in 1687.

In 1690 William used a certificate of importation to obtain a grant of 150 acres. This land was south of Puzzle Point Creek (now called New Mill Creek) on the Southern Branch of the Elizabeth River. This was in the area of the property of Jacob Smith.

Lower Norfolk County was a growing area and in 1691 was divided into Norfolk and Princess Anne Counties.

William filed a petition in the Court of Norfolk County in 1692 to assume custody and care of his mother-in-law, Elizabeth Smith, the widow of Jacob Smith. An excerpt of the petition which designates William as executor, reads:

It is ordered that the said William Whiddon take the said Elizabeth Smith home to his house and take care of her and nurse her as is fitting for her in her desecrated condition, and in consideration thereof the said Whiddon to have what land her said late husband Jacob Smith has and what property shall prove to be Smith's and the said Elizabeth's, she too shall continue with the said executor.

All of William's property was along the Southern Branch of the Elizabeth River.

A land grant was technically a long-term lease. An annual land tax, called Quit Rent, was due the crown for this lease. The Quit Rent Roll of 1704 shows William with 200 acres of property in Norfolk County.

The following Virginia property transactions for William were recorded:

1687	Purchased 50 acres from Jacob Smith.
1690	Used certificate of John to obtain 150 acres.
1692	Obtained property of Jacob Smith.
1701	With Ann, deeded land to Joseph Sugg.
1720	Willed 200 acres to son William.

William and Ann had the following children:

Name	Born	Spouse
John Whiddon		unknown
Thomas Whiddon		unknown
William Whiddon	ca. 1700	Dinah
Margaret Whiddon		Christopher Cawson

Thomas and William are on the Norfolk County list of tithables during the 1730s. A tithable refers to one who paid the capitation tax imposed by Virginia General Assembly. This tax was assessed on those considered to be productive members of society, including white males, Negro slaves and Indian servants all age sixteen or older.

John, William's oldest son, was witness in 1729 to a document by his cousin, Captain John Whiddon. This document provided gifts of land and slaves to the children of Captain Whiddon's second wife, Abigail

Church Cawson. John signed as John Whiddon Jun., which was common practice when signing for a relative of the same name.

Thomas, William's second son, died in 1736. An administrative bond was filed 18 March 1736 in Norfolk County for Thomas Whiddon, shipwright, deceased.

William made his will in 1720; it is fragmented and reads in part:

William Whiddon Sen.
Dated 18 Feb. 1720
Proved 16 June 1721, by Wm. Maunde & Wm. Gray

> *...unto my Son Wm. Whiddon my plantcon where on I now live, and a hundred and fifty ackers of land Called by the name of the Little ragg the sd. lands the whole Containing two hundred Ackers.....if in Care my Son....Sauld not make Sale of the sd. land in his life time and he Should... dye without heir or Issue then to fall to my Cosen John Whiddon Sen and male heirs....unto....Margaret Cason....Appoint my Son Wm. Whiddon and my Cosen John Whiddon...Exors*

> *Witnesses:*
> *George Sugg*   *Wm. Whiddon & Seal*
> *Wm. Maund*
> *Wm. Gray*

William's wife, Ann, and sons, John and Thomas, are not mentioned in the will. Ann apparently predeceased William and the older sons probably had already received their portion of William's land.

The other two children were mentioned in the will of their father. William received 200 acres of property from his father. Margaret was married at this time, as she is mentioned as Margaret Cason (Cawson).

An inventory of the estate of William Whiddon, Sr., deceased, was dated 15 Sep 1722. This document was signed by William Whiddon, Jr., making his mark.

Third Generation
William Whiddon

William, grandson of the Immigrant, was born about 1700 in Norfolk County, Virginia, and died about 1780 in Nash County, North Carolina. At the beginning of the 18th century Norfolk County was a bustling place. The Elizabeth River was constantly filled with ships, as shipbuilding and ocean trade were booming. Vacant land was quickly being taken by large landholders, who were acquiring more land for the expansion of their plantations.

When William was about twenty years old he inherited 200 acres of land from his father. This land lay on the Southern Branch of the Elizabeth River in the area of New Mill Creek.

The list of tithables of Norfolk County for 1730 through 1734 and in 1736 placed William's property in the Western Branch precinct. In 1736 he was listed with two tithables: himself and a Negro slave named Abraham.

The following Virginia property transactions for William were recorded:

1720 Obtained 200 acres from his father's will.

1723 16 Jan, purchased property from John Mercer.

1727 15 Mar, sold 100 acres to Captain John Whiddon for the sum of five shillings.

1745 14 Mar, with Dinah, sold 250 acres to John Southerland for 35 pounds.

1749 Sold 100 acres to Captain John Whiddon near the head of Southern Branch.

In the 1745 sale of property to John Southerland, both William and his wife are listed as sellers. Her name was Dinah, her last (maiden) name being unknown. Both signed the deed with their marks: William signed with a W and Dinah with an X.

William had the following children:

Name	Born	Spouse
Lott Whiddon R.S.	ca. 1730	Myra & Sarah
John Whiddon	ca. 1753	unknown
William Whiddon R.S.	ca. 1755	Mary Eason
Sarah Whiddon	ca. 1758	Marcum Cooper
Noah Whiddon R.S.	ca. 1760	Sheba McNeese

The age difference between Lott and his siblings indicates at least two wives for William. The only reference we have to Dinah is the 1745 deed, which places her between the two families of William. It is not known whether Dinah was the mother of Lott or of the second family.

About 1750 William decided to leave Virginia and move to North Carolina; he was part of a larger migration out of Virginia. Small to medium sized property owners were being squeezed out. When land was no longer productive, due to over farming of tobacco, expansion was not possible because of the unavailability of affordable land. With land becoming scarce in Virginia and being cheap and abundant in North Carolina, it seemed the natural thing to do. When King George II took control of North Carolina from the heirs of the Lords Proprietors in 1729, he eased purchase requirements and actively sought people to purchase land and move into North Carolina. Between 1730 and the Revolutionary War the population of North Carolina increased almost eightfold. William, along with his son Lott and others in the family, moved to Edgecombe County in North Carolina.

The migration out of Virginia included families with long histories in Norfolk County. Names familiar along the Elizabeth River, like Markham, Herbert, Cooper, Langley, Etheridge, Nash, Hall, Butt, Tucker and Griffin were becoming familiar in Edgecombe County.

William and his son Lott are listed on the Edgecombe County Muster Roll of 1750. They served in Captain Benjamin Lane's Company.

All able-bodied men between the ages of 16 and 60 were required to serve in the militia.

William's second family began in Edgecombe County with the birth of John about 1753 and William about 1755. Sarah and Noah followed in short order. The four siblings were born and raised in Edgecombe County.

William settled into life as a farmer acquiring land along Sapony Creek on Stoney Branch. His first North Carolina land purchase was in 1751. Over time he acquired a large amount of property, much more than he could have had in Virginia and became fairly prosperous. Edgecombe County provided relatively flat, heavily forested, well-drained land with the major agricultural crops being wheat, corn and tobacco.

The following North Carolina property transactions for William were recorded:

1751 19 Aug, purchased 91 acres from Green Hill on Sapony in Edgecombe County.

1752 12 Oct, received a warrant for 690 acres on Sapony Creek, Edgecombe County.

1754 30 Sep, purchased 100 acres from Lewis Perritt on NW side of Sapony Creek.

1754 30 Sep, purchased 200 acres from Lewis Perritt on N side of Sapony Creek.

1762 9 Mar, received a warrant for 700 acres in Edgecombe County.

1765 Purchased 450 acres from John Strickland.

1768 Sold the same 450 acres to Joshua Pearce.

1776 30 Jan, sold 91 acres to Marcum Cooper in the fork of Sapony Creek.

1776 30 Jan, conveyed 200 acres to John Whiddon on N side of Sapony Creek.

1779 14 Oct, conveyed 100 acres to William Jr. on NW side of Sapony Creek.

As counties became more populated over time they were subdivided into more manageable sized units. A petition to divide a growing Edgecombe County into three new counties was signed by William Whiddon and his son, John. The area in which they lived became Nash County. It was named for General Francis Nash, who had been mortally wounded while fighting under General George Washington during the American Revolution. Nash County was formed in 1777 from the western part of Edgecombe County.

After purchasing large tracks of land between 1751 and 1765 William began to sell off his property and beginning in 1776, at an advanced age, he dispersed his remaining property to his children.

Lott, William's oldest son, was a Revolutionary War soldier serving in the Halifax District Militia. He died on 28 December 1784 in Nash County. The inventory of his estate provides insight into colonial life in Edgecombe County:

> 2 head of horses, 13 head of cattle, 4 head of hogs, feather beds and furniture, 5 pewter dishes, 3 pewter basins, 5 pewter plates, 14 pewter spoons, 1 chest, 1 table loom, 4 slays, 1 pair of harness, 1 pair of hand mill stones, 1 woolen wheel, and 1 linen wheel, 3 iron pots and skillet, 1 butter pot, 1 griddle, 1 frying pan, 1 hand saw and half a whipsaw, 2 augers and 1 hammer, 1 gimlet, 1 pot rack, 1 iron box, 1 beef hook, 1 pair of sheep shears, 1 looking glass, 3 bedsteads, 1 tub, 2 pitchers, 1 meal sifter, 2 deer skins, 6 head of sheep, 1 cart and wheels, 2 pair of cotton cards, 2 bushels of salt, 1 plow hoe, 3 broad hoes, 3 grubbing hoes, 2 axes, 1 gun and shot bag, 4 tan cowhides, 16 geese, 2 hogs head and 1 barrel, 2 sides of leather, 1 meal stand, 20 barrels of corn, 2 stacks of books, 2 bells, 7 shears, 1 sack of specie money; 10L, 10s, 4d, and sundries act.

John, William's second son, died in Tattnall County, Georgia, in 1819.

Noah, William's youngest son, was a Revolutionary War soldier. He applied for a pension in 1832 from Butler County, Alabama.

Sarah, William's only daughter, married Marcum Cooper. Marcum was a witness on numerous legal documents for the Whiddon family.

Fourth Generation
William Whiddon R.S.

William, a Revolutionary War soldier, was born about 1755 in Edgecombe County, North Carolina. He married Mary Eason, probably in 1779, who was born about 1760. Their life together was one of hard work and self reliance. They were pioneers, living in sparsely populated areas of North Carolina, South Carolina and Georgia.

Large families were the norm for pioneer life. Children provided the labor that sustained the family, and they learned to work as soon as they were old enough. Boys worked in the field and tended the animals. Girls were taught to spin, weave cloth and sew. Clothes were homemade, using cotton grown on the farm and wool that was purchased. Work began before sunrise and ended long after sunset.

William and Mary had the following children:

Name	Born	Spouse
Eli Whiddon	ca. 1780	Dicy
Elizabeth Whiddon	1782	Nathan B. Barwick
Eleanor Whiddon	ca. 1783	James Barwick
Dempsey Whiddon	ca. 1784	Martha Rhoda Barwick
Sherrod Whiddon	ca. 1785	unknown
Winnaford Whiddon	ca. 1788	unknown
Feraby Whiddon	ca. 1790	Lewis Moore
William E. Whiddon	1794	Sarah Skinner
Lott Whiddon	1796	Judith Dorminy
John Whiddon	1799	Elizabeth Ferguson
Susannah Whiddon	1803	John J. Barwick

There is some dispute among Whiddon Family researchers regarding whether William married Mary Eason or Mary Davis. I believe the facts strongly support Mary Eason as the wife of William. Mary Eason was the daughter of William Eason, Jr. and Sarah Manning. Mary's father died in 1763, and her mother married Thomas Richardson, who, in 1779, owned land on the north side of Sapony Creek. This puts Mary Eason in close proximity to William, who also owned land on Sapony Creek. The 1783 will of William Eason, Sr. included his granddaughter Mary Whiddon. Also, a long connection existed between the Eason and Whiddon families; William Eason, Sr., William Eason, Jr. and William's father and brother Lott all served together in the militia in the 1750s. Further support for Mary Eason as William's wife is the pattern of names used by the Whiddon family, including Eli, Dempsey and Winnaford, which were found in the Eason family prior to the marriage of William and Mary. In addition, Gus Adams, who wrote genealogical articles for the *Tifton Gazette*, stated in his 1912 article on the Whiddon family that William's wife was Mary Eason. His information came from first-person interviews with family members.

As war with England approached Edgecombe County joined the movement to support independence; however, the county contained a large number of persons who remained loyal to the crown. This often pitted neighbor against neighbor. The Llewelyn conspiracy of 1777 was the largest loyalist plot in North Carolina in the war's early years. It was reported that in Edgecombe County, "many evil persons had joined in a wicked conspiracy". In July of that year, about thirty men tried to overrun Tarboro but were captured by local patriots. Edgecombe County provided less than wholehearted support for those who fought for independence during the American Revolution.

A military pay record for William Whiten, serving in the militia for the Wilmington Military District, may represent the only available record of William's actual service.

The State of North Carolina entered a warrant on 15 June 1779 for 1,000 acres to William for his service in the Revolutionary War. This parcel was to be in Nash County, bounded by the properties of Isham Gandy, Kent, Whitfield, John Whiddon, Evans, Cooper, Brinkley Gandy and William Whiddon, Sr. When the survey was completed, a tract containing 690 acres was issued on 10 November 1779. This tract was on the north side of Sapony Creek between Little Sapony Creek and Ready Branch.

William became prosperous and was a major landholder in Nash County. The 1782 Nash County tax list shows that William owned 1,700 acres of land, four slaves, three horses/mules, twenty head of cattle and personal property all valued at 450 pounds.

Besides his responsibility on his farm William was very busy with county affairs. In 1778 William and his brother Lott helped repair the road between the courthouse and the Tar River. William served as county assessor in 1779, as a patroller of Captain Hatton's district and often as a juror. In April of 1782 he was appointed Constable in place of Brinkley Gandy and in July he served as assessor in Captain Davenport's district for which he was paid 35 pounds. In January of 1783 William was appointed Constable in place of Simon Smith.

The following North Carolina property transactions for William were recorded:

1779 15 Jun, received warrant for 690 acres on N side of Sapony Creek.

1779 24 Aug, purchased 212 acres from Oswell Langley on N side of Sapony Creek.

1779 14 Oct, William Sr. conveyed to him 100 acres on NW side of Sapony Creek.

1780 Purchased 360 acres from William Worrell in the fork of Sapony Creek.

1780 10 Mar, purchased 100 acres from Isham Gandy on Little Sapony Creek.

1780 1 Apr, purchased 300 acres from Thomas Whitfield on S side of Ready Branch.

1782 3 Jun, purchased 112 acres from Matthew Brantley on S side of Sapony Creek.

1782 16 Jun, sold 212 acres to Brinkley Gandy located on S side of Sapony Creek.

1783 2 Oct, with Mary, sold 360 acres to Parson Rackley in fork of Sapony Creek.

1784 28 Dec, purchased 187 acres from Isham Gandy on N side of Little Sapony Creek.

1785 4 Jan, with Mary, sold 112 acres to Peter Ballard on S side of Sapony Creek.

1786 30 Mar, conveyed 77 acres to Noah Whiddon.

1787 13 Jan, sold 80 acres to Noah Whiddon on S side of Ready Branch.

1787 3 Feb, sold 300 acres to John Evans on S side of Ready Branch.

1788 8 Jan, sold 1,077 acres to Micajah Thomas located on Little Sapony Creek.

In 1783 William and Mary Whiddon sold 360 acres to Parson Rackley; this was the first time her name appeared on a legal document. In 1788 they sold the remainder of their property in Nash County in preparation of a move further south. The following is from Nash County Deed Book 1; it describes the final sale of property prior to William and Mary taking their family to South Carolina:

> William Whiddon of Nash Co. to Micajah Thomas of same, Jan. 8, 1788, for 600 pds. a track of 100 acres on the northwest side of Sapony Creek conveyed from Lewis Perret to Wm. Whiddon, Sr., and conveyed by him to Wm. Whiddon, Jr. on Oct. 14, 1779; also another track of 690 acres granted to Wm. Whiddon, Jr. by the State of N.C.; a third track of 287 acres granted to Isham Gandy by the State and conveyed by him to Wm. Whiddon, Jr. in two separate deeds, one dated March 10, 1780 and the other Dec. 28, 1784, the three tracks being on Little Sapony Creek adjoining Noah Whiddon, Marcum Cooper's path, John Evans, Kent (then Holland), and Cotise. Wit: Marcum Cooper, S. Westray, and Solomon Cotten.

After the final sale of their land in 1788 William and his family, along with his cousin Maxwell, loaded their wagons and headed south to find a new home in the Cheraw District of South Carolina. The journey was arduous, involving travel over rough roads, where they even existed and with highwaymen being a constant threat. William, Maxwell and their families no doubt traveled in a caravan with others going south.

In 1769 the South Carolina Assembly acted to create seven judicial districts, including the Cheraw District. A courthouse and jail were built at Long Bluff on the Pee Dee River to administer Cheraw District affairs. Prior to this all deeds, estate settlements and other legal matters had to go to Charleston to be recorded. The part of Cheraw District where William settled would in time become known as Darlington County.

In December of 1788 two parcels of land in the Cheraw District were surveyed for William Whiddon. Both contained 200 acres; one was on the north side of Black Creek and the other on Beaver Dam Creek. The grants for these properties were made to William in 1791 and 1793. The Darlington Courthouse burned in 1806, with most records of land transactions prior to that time being lost.

The following South Carolina property transactions for William were recorded:

1791 12 Apr, granted 200 acres on N side of Black Creek.
1793 6 Sep, granted 200 acres on Beaver Dam waters of Black Creek.
179? Purchased 490 acres from Amos Windham on Sparrow Swamp & Jump Gully.
1807 16 Jul, with Mary, sold 360 acres to Charles Beasley on Sparrow Swamp.
1807 19 Dec, sold 200 acres to Thomas Coker on W side of Boggy Swamp.
1808 26 Jan, with Mary, sold 100 acres to John Beasley.
1808 16 Feb, with Mary, sold 150 acres to Stephen Thompson on Sparrow Swamp.
1813 8 Jun, sold 170 acres to Charles Beasley on Sparrow Swamp & Jump Gully.
1814 10 Jun, sold 450 acres on Sparrow & Jump Gully.

After initially settling on Black Creek William moved a little farther south, when he procured 490 acres from Amos Windham on Sparrow Swamp. All of his land afterward was in the Lynches River/Sparrow Swamp area. William and Mary obviously purchased a large amount of land before 1806, based on the more than 1,400 acres they sold beginning in 1807. Living along Sparrow Swamp they became neighbors and friends with the Barwick family. There were four marriages between the children of William Whiddon and William Barwick.

A petition on behalf of the people of Darlington County for a road from the courthouse on the Pee Dee River to cross Black Creek at John Powell's Bridge and continuing to McCullam's Ferry on Lynches Creek was drafted on 2 November 1796. This petition, addressed "To the Honorable the President and Members of the Senate of the State of South Carolina", had more than eighty signers including William Whiddon and his oldest son, Eli.

Another petition (date unknown) on behalf on Darlington County inhabitants was signed by William Whiddon. The petition was for a bridge at Skinner's Landing and a road from the landing connecting to the road from Darlington Courthouse to McCullam's Ferry on Sparrow Swamp.

War loomed as tensions grew between America and Great Britain. American outrage at the impressments of American sailors into the British navy and British interference with American foreign trade caused war to be declared on 18 June 1812. The following is excerpted from a newspaper article published in the *City Gazette* on 11 September 1812:

Darlington Public Meeting.

At a meeting of a respectable number of the citizens of Darlington District, at Darlington Court-House, on the 18th day of July, 1812, Col. Lamuel Benton, was called to the chair, and Col. William Zimmerman, was appointed secretary, and the following gentlemen, to wit: - James Ervin, Major George Bruce, Cornelius Mandaville, Major William Williams, Moses Sanders, Josiah Cantey, Albert Fort, Andrew Hunter, Benjamin Skinner, John Norwood, sen. William Whiddon, John Huggins and Jeremiah Belk, were appointed a committee to draught a preamble and resolutions, approbatory of the declaration of War against Great Britain, who reported the following, which were unanimously adopted.

To avenge insult and repel injury is characteristic of a great and magnanimous people; to suffer them with impunity, bespeaks pusillanimity and invites to repetition. Great Britain, compelled to acknowledge us independent, has always manifested toward us a spirit of hostility. No sooner had she signed the treaty of eighty-three than she determined to evade it;…….

The preamble and resolves are lengthy and indicate strong feelings against the British and an ability to express them as eloquently as the founding fathers had done a generation earlier. Copies were sent to the president of the United States and to their delegate in Congress.

William and Mary were preparing to leave South Carolina when they sold the last of their property in 1814. On June 10 of that year, they sold 450 acres to Elias DuBose, Sr. and Elias P. Muse for $4,000.00. This brought to a close William and Mary's sojourn in South Carolina. They again packed their belongings and moved to Emanuel County, Georgia, along with their daughter, Elizabeth, and her husband, Nathan Barwick.

Emanuel County is located in the northern part of Georgia's Pine Barren region. The land is flat, with sandy soil, covered with pine forests and a carpet of wiregrass. Two major rivers flow through Emanuel County, both with Indian names: the Canoochee and the Ohoopee. Remnants of the Creek Indians were still in the county in the early 19th century. In 1828 an English soldier was touring the area and described roads as being almost nonexistent. Roads that existed were poorly marked and often impassable; yet he found the area to be one of quiet beauty.

A warrant requiring a survey for 550 acres of land, on Big Ohoopee River, was issued on 21 September 1815 by Emanuel County for William Whiddon. Under the headright system of granting land, the head of a family was entitled to 200 acres plus an additional 50 acres for each family member or slave. This land became the new home of William and Mary and their younger children. The official land grant was issued in 1820, two years after William's death.

William established a cotton farm on this property where he lived and worked until his death in 1818. On 24 November 1818 his son, Eli, applied for a letter of administration for William's estate. On 4 January 1819, the Inferior Court of Emanuel County appointed Eli administrator. The estate appraisal was recorded on 13 February 1819 and soon afterward the estate sale was conducted by Eli. The following was recorded regarding the sale of William's estate property:

The amount of the property of William Whiddon, deceased sold by Eli Whiddon administrator of said estate.

1	cow and yearling	to Warren Key	27.75
1	lot of plows	to Lott Whiddon	4.00
1	lot of plows	to Kinchin Jewell	4.00
1	grubbing hoe & wedge spade	to Kinchin Jewell	5.06
1	spade	to Elijah Beasley	1.31
2	hides	to William Beasley	2.56
1	lot of geese	to Elijah Beasley	4.15
1	woolen wheel	to Kinchin Jewell	4.06
1	woolen wheel & cards	to Mary Whiddon	.50
1	lot of coopers wax	to Mary Whiddon	1.00
1	lot of coopers wax	to Lott Whiddon	1.50
1	pot	to Kinchin Jewell	4.00
1	dutch oven	to John Brantley	.39
1	pot & 1 spider	to Mary Whiddon	1.00
1	kettle & griddle	to Mary Whiddon	1.00
1	chime keg & barrel	to Lott Whiddon	1.00
1	lot of chairs	to Mary Whiddon	1.50
1	table & shell ware	to Mary Whiddon	3.00
1	chest	to Mary Whiddon	1.00
1	musket & shot bag	to Lott Whiddon	6.06
1	rifle gun & shot bag	to John Whiddon	24.50
1	feather bed & furniture	to Mary Whiddon	10.00
100	lbs. seed cotton	to Thomas E. Ward	5.43
100	lbs. seed cotton	to Thomas E. Ward	5.56
200	lbs. seed cotton	to Mary Whiddon	6.00
100	lbs. seed cotton	to Warren Key	6.78
1	lot seed cotton @ 7 cents/lb.	to John Brantley	-----
1	Negro woman & children	to Mary Whiddon	1.00
6	head of hogs	to Mary Whiddon	6.00
1	bank of potato slips	to Lott Whiddon	4.37
1	stack of blade fodder	to Kinchin Jewell	12.00
1	lot of hogs at large	to John Brantley	10.00
1	pair (*unreadable*)	to Elijah Hakins	1.26

1	lot of corn	to Mary Whiddon	1.00
2	head of hogs	to Mary Whiddon	2.00
2	head of hogs	to Francis Meek	26.00
2	head of hogs	to Francis Meek	27.12
1	lot of hogs	to Lott Whiddon	26.00
1	club axe	to Ezekiel Smith	2.25
2	wagon bridles	to Thomas E. Ward	1.62
1	lathing axe	to Thomas E. Ward	.37
1	weeding hoe	to Aaron Gardner	.58
1	sifter meal tub & hot rack	to Mary Whiddon	1.00
1	lot of hogs	to William Beasley	9.00
1	lot of hogs	to Shadrick Kite	7.50

The widow was required to buy estate items just like anyone else, although it is obvious that she received deference based on the price she paid for her purchases. This is most obvious in the purchase of the Negro woman and her children for only $1.00.

The Georgia Journal and Messenger ran an advertisement placed by Eli Whiddon on 7 November 1820 that read as follows:

> *One woman about 25 years old, likely, an excellent house or field negro; one girl about six years old, active and liked; one boy about two years old, very lively—sold for the benefit of the heirs, Conditions of sale twelve months credit, with small notes and approved security.*

The following account of the sale was recorded in Emanuel County:

> *An account of the sale of the negroes belonging to the estate of William Whiddon deceased sold the 1st day January 1821.*

> | | |
> |---|---|
> | *1 woman named Matilda* | *$595.00* |
> | *1 girl named Jane* | *$361.00* |
> | *1 boy named Jared* | *$200.00* |
>
> *I certify the above to be truly stated.*
> *Eli Whiddon Admr*

The woman and her children whom Mary purchased for $1.00 at the estate sale in 1819 were sold for her by Eli for more than $1,000.00. This sale indicates that Mary was no longer living on her farm. The 1820 and

1830 census records show that she was living with daughter Elizabeth and her husband, Nathan Barwick.

Mary was granted land under the Georgia Land Lottery system based on being a widow of a Revolutionary War soldier. She was living in Emanuel County, Chasons Military District, and in 1821 she received 202½ acres in Henry County and in 1827 she received 202½ acres in Coweta County. There is no indication that Mary took possession of either; she probably sold them. There is a record in Coweta County of Mary Whitten selling land to Samuel Benton; this may be the land she had been granted in 1827. (Georgia used a lottery system to distribute the land taken from the Cherokee and Creek Indians.)

Mary died sometime after 1830 and was buried in the Barwick cemetery with her husband William. The cemetery is located near Norristown, Georgia. The tombstone is still there and reads "William Whitten and wife".

Tombstone of William and Mary Whiddon, Emanuel County, GA

Fifth Generation
Eli Whiddon

Eli was born about 1780 in Nash County, North Carolina. As a young boy, he moved with his family to South Carolina in 1788. He met Dicy, whose last name is not known, and they married, probably in 1796 or 1797. She, also, was born about 1780.

An old Whiddon Family Bible indicates that Eli's middle name was Green. This is the only known source that gives him a middle name. If, in fact, his name was Eli Green Whiddon he may have been named after the Revolutionary War hero General Nathanael Greene who had commanded the Southern Army and was greatly admired in North Carolina.

In November of 1796 Eli and his father signed a petition in Darlington County requesting the state provide a new road from the courthouse to Lynches Creek. Eli and Dicy are in the 1800 census of Darlington County with three children under age ten.

In the early 1800s Eli and Dicy moved south into Montgomery County, Georgia. Eli's brothers Dempsey and Sherrod moved along with them. This region was largely isolated from surrounding areas due to the scarcity of passable roads. Land was plentiful but the population gathered primarily along the county's rivers and streams. Most of the land remained vacant for decades. Life for settlers of this region, by any standard, was extremely difficult.

In 1804 Eli was residing in Georgia Military District 53 of the county and appears on a jury list. In 1805 and 1806 Eli appears on the county tax roll. On 3 March 1809 he was commissioned as a justice of the Inferior Court in Montgomery County. In 1810, 1811 and 1812 he was county tax collector. In 1811 he appeared on the county tax list as owning one slave and on the 1812 tax list as owning two slaves. Eli was on the militia rolls for the War of 1812, being part of the Tattnall & Montgomery Militia.

In 1812 Emanuel County was created from portions of Montgomery and Bulloch Counties. The area where Eli and Dicy lived became Emanuel County. The legislative act that created the new county appointed Eli Whiddon, Edward Lane, Francis Pugh, Needham Cox and Uriah Anderson the county commissioners. They were empowered to determine the site of the county's public buildings, contract for the building of a courthouse and jail and call elections.

Eli was elected to serve in the Georgia State House of Representatives from Emanuel County. He was a Representative during 1814, 1815 and 1816. In May of 1816 he was foreman of the Emanuel County Grand Jury.

Eli, like his father, received a grant for land on the Big Ohoopee River. He received 194 acres in December of 1815. Eli, who had been in the area for a decade, and his father, who had recently arrived, now lived in close geographic proximity.

Upon his father's death in 1818 Eli was appointed administrator of the estate. When the estate business was settled and his mother was safely ensconced in the home of his sister, Elizabeth, his feet began to itch again.

Eli was a winner in the 1820 Georgia Land Lottery while living in Emanuel County. He was granted 490 acres in Irwin County on 12 November 1822. Eli completed administering his father's estate in Emanuel County in 1821 and appeared in Florida in 1826. Between, he may have moved to Irwin County and, after a few years, sold this land and moved on to Florida. About 1826 Eli, Dicy and their family arrived in the Territory of Florida.

Florida became a United States Territory in 1821. Eli and his family initially settled in Gadsden County, which was created in 1823 as the territory's fifth county. In 1825 public land in Gadsden County was opened up for sale by the government.

Bennett, Matthew and Sevier, the three oldest sons of Eli and Dicy, all received land in the 1821 Georgia Land Lottery while living in Emanuel County. In 1826 all three made an application for land in Gadsden County, which was granted. Eli and his entire family made the move to Florida. After a brief stay in Florida, Eli purchased land in Decatur

County, Georgia, and made his home there. Decatur County, Georgia and Gadsden County, Florida, are adjoining counties and constitute one contiguous area.

In May of 1826 Eli purchased 250 acres located in District 21, lot number 369, from George W. King. This land was on the south bank of Mosquito Creek. In October of 1828 he purchased 250 acres from Elijah H. Callaway in District 21, lot 344. This parcel on the north bank of Mosquito Creek lay directly across from the earlier purchase. Elijah H. Callaway was Clerk of the Superior and Inferior Court of Emanuel County from 1818 to 1821. He was certainly known by Eli from his time in Emanuel County.

Decatur County was established in 1823, originally it was part of Early County. The county was named for Commodore Stephen Decatur, an American naval officer notable for his heroism in the Barbary War and the War of 1812. The soil and climate of the county were well suited for growing cotton and corn. Danger still existed from remnants of Indians who once dominated the region.

The following letter, dated 12 December 1826, was sent by the representatives of Decatur County to George M. Troup, Governor of Georgia. It was communicated to the Legislature on 19 December 1826:

> In consequence of the late ravages, and murders committed by the Indians; on our neighbors, the inhabitants of this creek (Tired Creek), and its vicinity, have collected and concluded to erect a temporary fortification for their present relief. We can raise thirty fighting men, and shall be able to make a tolerable stand against a small party of Indians. But our property will be exposed to the ravages of Indians. And our men are unorganized; without officers and of course without discipline. Unless we receive some immediate relief from your hands, our situation will be desperate our life exposed to the savage torture of the Indians and our property either burnt or destroyed

The following statement was made by the Decatur County Grand Jury in 1829:

> We present as a public grievance the residence of a number of Indians on or near the Flint River in the county who

are strolling through the county and, as we believe, do a considerable injury to the citizens generally, and not being governed by our laws, we view them as a public grievance and a pest to society.

In January 1827 Eli was listed in the Decatur County Superior Court records as a member of the Grand Jury.

After establishing a life in Decatur County with a thriving farm and a growing family, Eli died in 1834. He was about 54 years old and left Dicy with seven minor children.

Eli and Dicy had the following children:

Name	Born	Spouse
Bennett Whiddon	ca. 1797	unknown
Matthew Whiddon	ca. 1798	Ann Fain
Sevier Whiddon	1801	Matilda Smith & Kissiah Johnson
Mary Whiddon	ca. 1805	Ruben Meeks & Howard Cobb
Nancy Whiddon	ca. 1807	William M. Owens
John H. Whiddon	ca. 1810	never married
Eli Whiddon, Jr.	ca. 1815	Elizabeth
Elizabeth Whiddon	ca. 1818	James H. Gough & James W. Stanley
Louisa Whiddon	ca. 1820	Henry A. Lewis & Robert Nixon
Alexander Whiddon	ca. 1821	Elizabeth Johnson
William Whiddon	ca. 1825	Elizabeth McGowen
James Whiddon	ca. 1827	Mary Thomas
David Whiddon	ca. 1828	Martha Ann Caswell & Dicey Hayes

On 3 May 1834 the Decatur County Inferior Court granted letters of administration to Dicy Whiddon and John H. Whiddon for the estate of Eli Whiddon. Also, ordered by the court was an appraisal of the estate.

On 5 May a bond of $7,000.00 was posted by John H. and Dicy Whiddon and Bennett Crawford, requiring an inventory of Eli's estate. The bond was signed by John H., Dicy, with her mark, and Bennett Crawford.

The following is a partial list taken from the estate appraisal dated 23 June 1834. The complete inventory shows a prosperous farm and a well-furnished home. Total value of the property was estimated at $3,731.32:

12	head beef cattle	73.00
117	head stock cattle	409.00
1	yoke oxen & cart	50.00
14	books	
2	shotguns & 1 rifle	25.00
69	bee hives	103.50
7	beds &furniture	175.00
7	slaves	2100.00
28	head of hogs @ 1.00	28.00
2	square of land	500.00
199	apple trees & 73 peach trees	28.50

The estate sale was required by law to be advertised. The following ad was placed in *The Southern Recorder*:

> *John H, and Dicy Whiddon, Admrs. of Eli Whiddon estate, give notice to debtors and creditors, July 7, 1834; at the same time they advertise for sale the personal property of the estate at his late residence 1ˢᵗ Monday in Sept.*

On 22 April 1836 division of the estate was made to the heirs of Eli. Dicy and twelve children were to receive equal portions of the approximately $3,800.00 received from the sale. Bennett was not included among the heirs; he may have predeceased Eli.

On 5 January 1835 John H. was appointed guardian for the person and property of his brother Eli Jr. It was also ordered that the administrator of Eli Whiddon's estate would have leave to sell the land and Negroes of said estate.

In March of 1836 Louisa, Alexander and Elizabeth were allowed to choose their guardians because they were over the age of fourteen. Louisa and Alexander chose John H. as their guardian. Elizabeth chose her brother, Sevier. Dicy was appointed guardian for her three young sons William, James and David.

In 1842 the Florida Armed Occupation Act was passed to encourage the settlement of Florida. After the Second Seminole War the government passed the act, which was officially titled "An Act to Provide for the Armed Occupation and Settlement of the Unsettled Part of the Peninsula of East Florida". The act granted 160 acres of unsettled land to any head of a family under three conditions: first, the settler must be able to bear arms, second, he or his heirs must live on the land for five years and third, the settler must clear five acres and build a house within one year.

John H. Whiddon and his brother William both got the permits required to obtain land under the Florida Armed Occupation Act in May of 1843. Dicy decided to go with them. She and her son-in-law James H. Gough obtained permits in July of that year, but things do not always go as planned. Dicy died before she could go and William changed his mind and stayed in Decatur County. John H. Whiddon and James and Elizabeth Gough headed south and settled in what would become Sumter County, Florida.

James, the next-to-youngest son, either traveled with them or followed shortly thereafter. He married Mary Ann Thomas in Marion County, Florida, in 1846 and they eventually settled in Pasco County, Florida. The youngest son, David, remained in Decatur County.

John H. Whiddon, who never married, eventually moved to Tampa where he died in 1848. In his will he left $500.00 each to the American Tract Society of New York, the Methodist-Episcopal Tract Society (South), the Baptist Missionary Bible and Tract Society (South) and the Methodist-Episcopal Building Fund of Tampa. He left $1,000.00 and a Negro woman to his brother Eli. The rest of the estate was to be equally divided between his other ten siblings. The reason Eli received a greater portion of the estate may be based on a close relationship established when John H. assumed guardianship of Eli at the death of their father.

Sixth Generation
David Whiddon

David, the youngest son of Eli and Dicy, was born in 1828 in Decatur County, Georgia. His father died when he was only six years old and his mother died when he was fifteen. Following the death of David's mother some of his siblings moved to central Florida to obtain land under the Florida Armed Occupation Act, while others remained in Decatur County and the surrounding area. David was among the family members who remained in Decatur County.

David married Martha Ann Caswell on 7 December 1848. She apparently died, because he was married again, on 30 March 1851, to Dicey Hayes. Dicey was born about 1828 in Jasper County, Georgia. In the early 1830s she along with her widowed mother, Nancy, and siblings moved to Decatur County. (After arriving in Decatur County, Nancy Hayes married Michael Joyce in 1834. The marriage was short-lived; she was listed as the head of her household on the 1840 census. She continued using the Joyce surname for some time but eventually reverted to the name Hayes. Resuming the Hayes name returned her to the same surname as her children.)

David and Dicey had three children:

Name	Born	Spouse
Sarah J. Whiddon	1852	never married
James I. Whiddon	06 Jan 1854	Mary J. Lundy
Henry William Whiddon	26 Oct 1856	Letitia Martin

David lived in Decatur County until his untimely death in 1858. He left behind a widow and three young children. In August of 1858 Dicey was appointed administrator of David's estate. A bond of $800.00 was posted by Dicey Whiddon as principle, and her brothers Samuel N. and Elias D. Hayes as secondaries. Dicey signed the bond with her mark.

It was ordered by the Decatur County Court that Elihu Davis, Isaac Wilks, Bennett Whiddon, Samuel W. Patterson and James M. Hayes be appointed to appraise the estate of David Whiddon, deceased.

Appraisement of the estate of David Whiddon deceased:

6	split bottom chairs	6.00
2	common chairs	1.00
1	bedstead turned 4.00 & 1 pine bedstead 2.00	6.00
2	trunks	3.50
1	family Bible & 1 small Bible	2.00
	razor strap brush	1.00
1	steak dish .50, 1 pitcher .50, ½ dozen tumblers 2.50	3.50
1	large dish .50, 1 pitcher .50, 1 sugar dish .25	1.25
1	small pitcher .25, 1 salt cellar .50	.75
1	set plates .38, 1 candle stick .12	.50
1	broke set cups saucers	.37
1	set table & 1 set tea spoons	5.00
1	small table	1.00
4	large plates .25, 2 bowls & 1 pitcher .75	1.00
1	large mirror 2.00, 1 bell stand .05	2.05
	bed and fixings	40.00
	Trunk	2.00
1	set pots, ovens & cooking utensils	10.00
2	Buckets, 1 pair candle molds & bread tray	3.00
1	tin stand 1.00, 1 set grind stew fixings 1.00	2.00
1	axe hatchet, (unreadable) & padlock	1.75
	(unreadable) 1.00, 4 bed blankets 6.00	7.00
3	linen table clothes	5.00
4	sheets 2.00, 2 counterpanes 6.00	8.00
4	bed quilts 10.00, 1 bed quilt not quilted 2.00	12.00
3	head hogs	9.00
10	head stock cattle	50.00

After David's death, Dicey and her three children went to live with her mother. Nancy Hayes' household already included several of her unmarried adult children. The Hayes family was a large family, as Nancy had nine children. The Hayes children tended to marry late or not at all, which may have been to support their widowed mother. Dicey and her younger sister were the only ones who married at a young age, which was typical for the times.

On 5 November 1860 Dicey married John S. White and, shortly afterward, they moved to Jackson County, Florida. On 10 January 1861 John S. White was appointed guardian of Sarah, James and Henry by the Probate Court in Jackson County. On 14 January 1861 Decatur County appointed Samuel N. Hayes, Dicey's brother, as guardian of Sarah Jane Whiddon.

After being married about a year John and Dicey had a son named Stephen. Jackson County records show that John White married again in 1865 to Martha Dykes. This indicates that Dicey died between 1861 and 1865. She may have died when giving birth to Stephen.

By 1870 Sarah, James and Henry were in Decatur County, living with their uncle and aunt. They lived with Thomas and Martha Hayes, who were brother and sister, neither was married. Their grandmother, Nancy, was deceased by this time. These Whiddon children were fortunate to have the Hayes family to care for them.

Seventh Generation
Henry William Whiddon

Henry William was born in Decatur County, Georgia, on 26 October 1856. David, his father, died before Henry's second birthday and Dicey, his mother, died when he was between five and eight years old. He and siblings James and Sarah were raised by their maternal grandmother, Nancy Hayes. The Hayes family was a close-knit group and they kept David's children together.

After Grandma Nancy passed away the three Whiddon children continued to live with Thomas and Martha Hayes, Nancy's unmarried children. At the time of the 1870 census a domestic servant was listed as living with them. He was an eleven year old black male named Josh Hamilton. No doubt many young black children, separated from their parents during slavery, were without adult help and consequently worked for and lived with white families after the Civil War.

Henry William preferred his middle name and was called Will or Bill. In later life he picked up the nickname Devil Bill; we can only guess why.

His brother James married Mary Lundy in 1877 and started his own household; Sarah and Henry William lived with them. Also, in their house was their Aunt Martha, who had helped raise the Whiddon children. The 1880 census indicates that Sarah had a disability. This may be why she never married.

In the early 1880s Henry William went to Florida. The 1885 Florida census showed him in Orange County. He may have worked on the railroad or in the citrus industry, both of which were booming in Florida at the time.

In Orange County he met Letitia Martin. She had moved to Florida with her family from Liberty County, Georgia, where the Martin family had a long history in the Taylor's Creek area. She was born in Liberty County on 31 May 1865.

Henry William and Letitia were married on 6 June 1886. After a stay in Orange County they returned to Decatur County when he inherited land from his uncle, Elias D. Hayes who was a prosperous land holder. At his death Elias, who had no children, left his property to his niece Sarah and his three nephews. His nephews were James and Henry William Whiddon and Samuel C. Hayes, son of his brother, Samuel N. Hayes.

The farm that Henry William inherited was approximately 200 acres. It was located in the southwest corner of the county near the Flint River. Henry William raised corn, cotton and livestock on this property which was only a few miles from the property that Eli had purchased when he first came to the county in the 1820s. This is the longest period of time the family remained in one place since leaving Norfolk County, Virginia, in 1750.

Henry William and Letitia had the following children:

Name	Born	Spouse
Monica Whiddon	18 Apr 1887	Alto L. Johns
Lila Whiddon	ca. 1889	Eulus J. Martin
Jesse D. Whiddon	06 Jan 1891	Amanda C. Earnest
Frank M. Whiddon	13 Feb 1893	Minnie Lee Belk
Chester W. Whiddon	31 Mar 1895	Nora Clark
Samuel G. Whiddon	11 Nov 1897	
Catharine Georgia Whiddon	24 Sep 1899	
James C. Whiddon	05 Feb 1902	never married
Anna Marie Whiddon	29 May 1904	William T. Powell
Willie May Whiddon	10 Oct 1906	Robert M. Freeman

Letitia called Henry William, Will and she was called Tish. Their farm was about five miles from the Florida state line and the closest town was Chattahoochee, Florida.

Will died in Decatur County on 22 September 1922. He is buried in Mount Pleasant Cemetery in Gadsden County, Florida. His tombstone reads "an honest man, the noblest work of God".

After Will died Tish left the farm and moved to River Junction in Gadsden County. Tish's youngest daughter, May, and her husband, Robert Monroe Freeman lived with her. Tish died 30 September 1942 and is also buried in Mount Pleasant Cemetery. Her tombstone reads "a tender mother and faithful friend".

Eighth Generation
Jesse David Whiddon

Jesse was born 6 January 1891 in Decatur County, Georgia. He was the oldest son of Henry William and Letitia Whiddon. He grew up working on his father's farm when he was not in school.

On 14 February 1915 he married Amanda Clara Earnest in Decatur County. Amanda was the daughter of Marion Earnest and Amanda McCullers. She was born 7 September 1895 near Donaldsonville, Georgia on her family's farm. Donaldsonville was then located in Decatur County but became part of Seminole County when Seminole County was formed in 1920.

Jesse and Amanda had the following children:

Name	Born	Spouse
Jesse Winfred Whiddon	10 Feb 1916	Sarah Ann Hayes
Marshall Foye Whiddon	31 Aug 1917	Floriece Griffin
Hayes Louis Whiddon	25 Aug 1918	Wyolene Philmon
Marion May Whiddon	28 Dec 1919	Cullen L. Sykes
Myrna Merlin Whiddon	10 Jan 1925	William J. Dollar
Claude Ray Whiddon	29 Dec 1932	Inez Sheffield

In 1914 war had begun in Europe and inevitability America would be drawn into the conflict. America entered World War I in April of 1917. Jesse registered for the draft in June of that year; his registration card described him as short and slender with blue eyes and black hair. He was not called into service because he was married and had a child.

After Jesse and Amanda married, they rented land near Jesse's father and began their life together as farmers. Close to ten years later they decided to leave farming behind and find another way to support their growing family. Jesse became the first Whiddon of his line to leave the land and pursue an occupation other than farming.

In the early 1920s Jesse and Amanda moved to River Junction, near Chattahoochee in Gadsden County, Florida. River Junction was a major connecting point for railroads in the Florida panhandle. They bought a house on Morgan Avenue and Jesse took a job with the Florida Gravel Company as a crane operator. He unloaded barges, that contained gravel dredged from the bottom of the Flint River, into railroad cars. He worked for the company for nearly twenty years. He walked to work as he lived only a short distance, through a wooded area, from the gravel company. His youngest son, Ray, often met him after work and they walked home together.

For the second time in Jesse's life the world was at war. Asia was in chaos with Japan attacking China in 1937 and Hitler had set Europe ablaze by 1939. It was obvious that America would eventually be forced into combat. Success in war required a massive buildup of American military and industrial capability. War preparation created jobs and men were needed to fill them. The shipyard at Portsmouth, Virginia, needed a massive influx of manpower to support our navy. Jesse and Amanda moved to Virginia in 1941 for work in the shipyard. Their entire family, with the exception of son Marshall, followed them. After an absence of nearly 200 years the Whiddon family was again in Norfolk County, Virginia; they returned to the area where John Whiddon, the Immigrant first landed in 1635.

Jesse took a job in the shipyard as a crane operator, as the shipyard used many cranes to move all the material required in ship construction and repair. He worked in the salvage yard unloading scrap metal to be used in the construction of warships. This was similar to the work he had done for the Florida Gravel Company.

Jesse was required to register for the war as a man born between 1877 and 1897. His draft registration described him as 5'6" tall, weighing 160 lbs., with blue eyes and gray hair. He registered on 27 April 1942, the same day his grandson, Hayes Louis Jr., was born in his house. Jesse was never called to service in the military.

When the war was successfully concluded, Jesse felt the urge to return to more familiar surroundings. After five years in Virginia he and

Amanda returned to Florida. The rest of the family followed, except for Hayes, who remained in Virginia.

In 1946 Jesse moved to Chattahoochee, Florida, into a house on Water Street next to the ice house. He took a job at the Florida State Hospital, in the power plant, working as a boiler operator regulating coal input to the furnaces. He worked there until his death.

While working in his garden at his home on Decatur Street, Jesse suffered a heart attack. He died in the hospital in Chattahoochee on 15 April 1960. He is buried in Mount Pleasant Cemetery in Gadsden County. His grandsons served as pallbearers at his funeral.

After Jesse died, Amanda moved to Bainbridge, Georgia, to be near her daughter Myrna. Amanda died on 15 February 1977 in Huntsville, Alabama while visiting with her son Ray. She is buried beside her husband in Mount Pleasant Cemetery. She was known to her grandchildren as Mamo.

Jesse and Amanda, Norfolk County, VA, 1942

Ninth Generation
Hayes Louis Whiddon

Hayes Louis was born on 25 August 1918 near Donaldsonville, Georgia, on the farm of his maternal grandfather, Marion Earnest. He was called Louis, eschewing his first name. His maternal grandmother died in 1914 and Marion Earnest remarried the following year to Rhoda Jane Faircloth. Louis knew her as Grandma Janie.

Louis grew up in Chattahoochee, Florida. While attending high school he was co-captain, with his brother Marshall, of the basketball team. After graduation he went to work at the Florida State Hospital as an orderly and played on the local baseball team.

While working at the hospital, he met Wyolene Philmon, who was in nurse's training. She was born 12 February 1920 in Houston County, Georgia. Wyolene was the daughter of Shellie Philmon and Alma Irene Jones Philmon. In 1923 or 1924 the Philmons moved to Pasco County in central Florida. They were farmers their entire lives.

Part of Wyolene's training required specialized studies that were not available at the Florida State Hospital. She went to New Orleans for this training and while there she and Louis married. On 11 March 1940 they wed in secret because student nurses were forbidden to marry.

In January 1941 they left Chattahoochee and moved to Toccoa, Georgia, where Louis took a job with R.J. La Tourneau, Inc. as an inspector of earth-moving equipment, but the drumbeat of war was quickening.

The world changed radically on 7 December 1941. Japan attacked Pearl Harbor and America was again at war. Louis's brother Jesse wrote him a letter describing the opportunities for employment at the Norfolk

Naval Shipyard in Portsmouth, Virginia. People were being hired by the thousands. The letter included a job application from the shipyard.

After receiving Jesse's letter Louis and Wyolene headed north to Virginia. Upon their arrival in January 1942 they moved in with Louis' parents and immediately Louis began work in the shipyard located on the banks of the Elizabeth River. He was employed as a pipe coverer and insulator. Their first child, Hayes Louis Jr. was born in April 1942 at the home they shared with Louis' parents. This home was on Treakle Street in the Williams Court housing project. When housing was available Louis, Wyolene and Louis Jr. moved into a house of their own.

Shipbuilding was the nation's biggest wartime industry and during the course of the war, the shipyard in Portsmouth averaged the completion of either the overhaul or construction of three ships each day. By 1943 the employment level of the shipyard soared to almost 43,000 from a prewar level of less than 8,000.

Shortage of housing was a major concern with so many new people arriving in the area every day. Whole neighborhoods were constructed to house the thousands of new defense workers and their families. Many of these temporary homes continued to be occupied for 40 to 50 years.

It was a time of scarcity. Meat, butter, sugar, gasoline and other common commodities were rationed. The Whiddons' diet consisted of cabbage, rutabagas and other readily available vegetables.

In May of 1944 Louis was drafted and reported for duty at Fort McPherson in Atlanta. Army records list him as six feet tall. While he was away Wyolene, who was expecting their second child, went to stay with her parents in Pasco County, Florida. Louis received an honorable discharge in January 1945 for medical reasons.

Louis and Wyolene resumed their life in Virginia when Louis returned to the shipyard, where he became a supervisor. They lived in Williams Court, a government housing project, until buying a house on Francis Street in Portsmouth in 1954. While living in Williams Court a Baptist mission church was formed and Louis and Wyolene became charter members. This mission church eventually became Fairview Heights Baptist Church. Louis served as a deacon and Wyolene as a Sunday school teacher.

Louis and Wyolene had the following children:

Name	Born	Spouse
Hayes Louis Whiddon, Jr.	27 Apr 1942	Elaine Carlyle Carter
James Edward Whiddon	02 Jun 1944	Renée Glynn Vann & Brenda Perez
Janice Irene Whiddon	18 Dec 1954	Michael K. Piquette
Robert Lloyd Whiddon	23 Mar 1956	Crystal Ann Eaton

Their family continued to grow and life was normal until one day in 1973 when Louis began having difficulty breathing and went to the shipyard dispensary. The X-ray taken revealed he had contracted asbestosis, a disease caused by asbestos fibers scarring the lungs and reducing breathing capacity. Three decades of working with and around asbestos had taken its toll. His career at the shipyard was ended when he was involuntary retired on disability.

Whiddon was involved in lawsuits against the asbestos manufacturers and served as an expert witness in a number of cases. He watched coworkers die of this disease until virtually all were gone. He is one of the very few to survive, as his asbestosis remained dormant. He spent a great deal of time assisting the widows of his coworkers through the bureaucratic maze of filing for their government benefits.

At this writing Louis and Wyolene remain in good health and still reside in their home on Francis Street.

Louis, Wyolene and Junior, Norfolk County, VA, 1942

Part III

The Other Whiddon Lines of Descent

Line of Descent of John, Son of the Immigrant

John II

John Whiddon, the oldest son of the Immigrant, was born about 1644 in Lower Norfolk County, Virginia. It is probable that his father apprenticed as a shipwright with John Yates. John married Joan Yates, the granddaughter of John Yates and daughter of Richard Yates. John Whiddon and Joan Yates became the progenitors of a very prosperous family.

Shipbuilding was a major enterprise in 17th century Virginia. Many English ships were constructed along the Virginia waterways. The good quality and ready supply of timber coupled with the relatively low cost of labor made Virginia an excellent place to build ocean-going vessels. Richard Yates, of Lower Norfolk County, was among the principle shipwrights in Virginia.

Although John Whiddon married into a prominent shipbuilding family he was a cordwainer. In 1664 John was listed in the Bristol Register as an indentured servant. John was indentured to Darby Conner for a four-year period. (The Bristol Register was a record maintained in Bristol, England of the names of all indentured servants embarking to America, though some of those listed were already in the American colonies and not sailing from England.) John was established as a cordwainer before marrying Joan Yates.

The leather from Cordoba, Spain, called cordovan was known in England as cordwain. The English term cordwainer referred to a maker of fine footwear using cordovan leather. The London shoemaker's guild—the Worshipful Company of Cordwainers—helped finance Captain John Smith's 1607 expedition to Virginia and Smith was inducted into the guild himself. The first cordwainers in America came to Jamestown by

1610 and the Secretary of Virginia recorded a flourishing shoe and leather trade as early as 1616. By the 1660s the Virginia Assembly directed that each county must erect a tannery and a shoe manufactory. The Assembly also imposed tariffs on leather and shoes exported from Virginia.

John Yates died before 1648 leaving his estate to his wife, Johanna. Her will in 1663 bequeathed 150 acres and an orchard to granddaughter Joan Yates. The use of Joan's maiden name indicates that she and John Whiddon were not yet married. In his will of 1678 Richard Yates bequeathed a gun to his son-in-law John Whiddon, a cow and calf to grandson John Whiddon and a calf to granddaughter Joan Whiddon so it is clear that John Whiddon and Joan Yates were married and had two children between 1663 and 1678.

The next account of John we find occurs in 1673 when he is on the importation list of John Porter. In 1675 he purchased land from Isaac Seaborne, shipwright, and used his own certificate of importation in 1678 to obtain an additional 300 acres. His properties were numerous and located along the Southern Branch of the Elizabeth River, between Deep Creek and Great Bridge.

In 1692 the rights to 150 acres were conveyed to John and his children. The land came from Joan's two living sisters and their husbands. The failure to mention Joan Whiddon on this deed indicates that she was deceased at this time. John married again to Elizabeth, whose last name is unknown.

John appears on the 1704 Quit Rent Roll in Norfolk County as possessing 420 acres. The Quit Rent was a tax of one shilling per fifty acres that landowners paid to the king. In 1708 John deeded the property that he lived on to his only son. John was identified as a cordwainer on this deed.

John died probably in 1709 and his widow, Elizabeth, was named as executrix. By 1710, she was also deceased, and John III petitioned for the release of funds from the estate to cover burial costs of his father and Elizabeth. An inventory of John's estate dated 6 March 1710 was witnessed by his son, Jonas Cawson and John Portlock. The inventory included shoe-making tools, powering tubs, lye tubs and six hides of leather.

John III

John Whiddon, grandson of the Immigrant, was born about 1675 in Lower Norfolk County, Virginia. Although his father practiced the trade of cordwainer, John born into a seafaring society decided to look toward the sea for his livelihood. He followed the example of his grandfather, Richard Yates. Many of his neighbors such as the Herberts, Seabornes and Ethridges were captains or shipwrights. John III was both a captain and a shipwright.

The following was recorded on 21 December 1722 in the Norfolk County Court: "Joseph Richardson an orphan bound as apprentice to Capt. John Whiddon to teach him the art of shipwright".

Captain John Whiddon inherited a great deal of property and in 1717 he received a patent for an additional 119 acres on the west side of the Southern Branch of the Elizabeth River in Elizabeth River Parish. He obtained a number of other properties during his lifetime to add to his holdings. He was a very wealthy man.

John married Elizabeth, whose last name is unknown. They had one child, a daughter named Mary who was born about 1710. She married Captain Markham Herbert, oldest son of Captain Thomas Herbert.

Captain Whiddon was a witness to the will of Captain Thomas Herbert in 1749. This will in part states: "Unto my eldest son Markham Herbert the plantation whereon I now live and the land belonging to it and one copper still now standing on my plantation. Twelve leather chairs, one gun, a bayonet, a pair of pistols and a back sword". The Whiddons married into wealth, adding to their level of affluence.

Elizabeth, John's wife, died in 1727. John married Abigail Church Cawson in 1729. She was the widow of his good friend Jonas Cawson. After their marriage, he made a Deed of Gift to the children of the late Jonas Cawson. He gave Cawson's plantation to the oldest son, Christopher, and gifts of slaves to the other Cawson children. Captain John Whiddon and Abigail had two children, John and Martha. John was born in 1730 and Martha in 1731.

Norfolk County required a new courthouse and in 1726 Captain John Whiddon and Peter Malbone were contracted to build it on the site of the existing courthouse on Main Street in Norfolk. Malbone was to build the courthouse and Captain John Whiddon was the financial backer of the venture. Whiddon received payment of 35,000 pounds of tobacco as his part of the transaction.

Captain John Whiddon is listed among the tithables for Norfolk County in 1731 and 1732 in Indian Creek Canton with Christopher Cawson, William Wallis and eight slaves, a total of 11 tithables each year. In 1733 he is charged with 14 tithables. In 1735 and 1736 he is in the Ferry Point to Great Bridge district with 6 and 7 tithables.

Captain John Whiddon died in 1750 and left the following will:

Lower Norfolk County
9 Nov 1748
Proved 10 January 1750

IN THE NAME OF GOD AMEN I John Whiddon of Norfolk County in Virginia being sick and weak but in sound and perfect sense and memory praised be Almighty God for it but knowing it is appointed to all men once to die do make and ordain this to be my Last Will and Testament in manner and form as followith: First I bequeath my Soul to Almighty God and the Lord Jesus Christ that give it and my body to the Earth to be buried in a decent manner as my executors hereafter named shall think fitt and for all my Worldly goods as well as personal after all just debts paid I do give and bequeath in manner and form as follows—

ITEM I give and bequeath to my Daughter Mary Herbert wife of Markcom Herbert the Dividend of Land with the Plantation thereon that I bought and purchased of William Ballantine Lying on the South side of Bay Tree Hole to her and her Heirs for ever being the same Land I have already made over to the said Markcom Herbert by and acknowledged in the open Court of Norfolk. I also give to my Said Daughter Mary Herbert one negro man called Sam also one negro woman called Cabe with her increase all which she is and hath been possessed with I also give to my Said Daughter Mary Herbert one heifer at my decease it being in full her portion.

ITEM I give and bequeath to my Daughter Martha Whiddon one Hundred acres of Land with the Plantation thereon Lying on the North Side of the Western Branch of the Elizabeth River being the Land formerly Mossets which Said Land I give to her and her Heirs forever and in case an Heir shall come and disinherit my Said Daughter of the Said Land then my will is that my Said Daughter Martha Whiddon shall have one Hundred acres of Land with the Plantation which I bought of William Whiddon to her and her Heirs for ever I also give to my Daughter Martha Whiddon four Negroes in this order; Sarah George Chinea and Hannah to her and her Heirs for Ever and the increase of the Said three girles I also give to my Said Daughter one feather bed Furniture.

ITEM I give and bequeath unto my Son John Whiddon the house and Plantation with the Woodland Grounds thereunto Belonging to which I now Live on also fourteen acres of Land joining thereon called Pedley's I also give to my Said Son John Whiddon Three negro men viz, George Ceaser James also a negro boy named Sam also I give to my Son John Whiddon one negro Woman named Lemon and five girls viz, Nanny Dinah Easter Lemon and Pleasant them with their increase to him and his Heirs for Ever only reserving to my Loving wife Abigail Whiddon the use of the negroes and Estate with privileges of the house and Plantation I now Live on during her natural Life and after her decease as before Said to my Son John Whiddon and his Heirs for Ever But if it should please God that my Daughter

Martha Whiddon should Die before she attains to the years of twenty one or marry then and in such case her Estate both Real and Personal to fall to my Son John Whiddon and his Heirs for Ever and if it should please God that my Son John Whiddon should Die before he attain to the age of twenty years at which time I allow him of age or marry then and in such a case his estate both real and personal after my wife's decease to be equally divided between my two Daughters viz, Mary Herbert and Martha Whiddon them and their Heirs for Ever and for the true performance of this my Last Will and Testament I do hereby appoint and nominate my Loving Wife Abigail Whiddon and my Son John Whiddon wholly and jointly my Executrix and Executor in Witness whereof I have hereunto set my hand and fixed my Seal this 9th day of November Anno Domi 1749.

Signed & Sealed in the presence of us
Wm Bayley
Paul Ballentine   John Whiddon & Seals
Anna Ballentine her mark   His mark

John IV

John Whiddon, great grandson of the Immigrant, was born 19 September 1730 in Norfolk County, Virginia. He inherited a great deal of wealth from his father. John was an astute businessman and added considerably to his inherited fortune. He was a shipbuilder and ship owner.

He married Elizabeth Nicholas, daughter of Captain John Nicholas, and they had two children. The oldest child, Rebecca married John Edwards in 1766. John V, the only male heir, married Ann Herbert in 1772. Elizabeth died in 1757.

John married again in 1758 to Mary Corprew. She was the daughter of Joshua and Elizabeth Corprew. John and Mary had six children. The first was Elizabeth, who married Captain William Cunningham in 1778. Second was Mary, who married Dr. Ludowick Broadie in 1782. (Dr. Broadie was a surgeon for the Virginia Militia during the Revolutionary War and for his service he received a grant of 6,000 acres in Mecklenburg County, Virginia.) John and Mary's other two surviving children were Martha, who married John Massenburg, and Ann, who married John Peters in 1787. John and Mary also had two children, Abigail and Joshua Corprew, who died in infancy.

Norfolk County tithable records show that John Whiddon was among the wealthiest men in the county. The tithables list him in the Ferry Point to Great Bridge district. In 1751 he had four slaves and by 1759 he had 14. The 1765 tithables show him as a man of substantial holdings. He owned more than 1,200 acres, 19 slaves and a carriage. Ownership of a carriage was rare in the county. The 1770s tithables continued to show him to be a man of wealth with large land holdings and as many as 23 slaves. Compared to others on the tithables, John Whiddon was one of the largest landowners and slave holders in the county during this period.

The county was growing and in 1761 the General Assembly at Williamsburg divided the Elizabeth River Parish into three parishes. One of these created parishes was St. Bride's Parish which covered the area between the Eastern and Southern Branches of the Elizabeth River and included the southern part of the county. John Whiddon was vestryman of St. Bride's Parish in 1767 with John Corprew and in 1771 with William Happer.

A newspaper advertisement in the 29 January 1767 edition of the *Virginia Gazette* advertised the sale of a vessel of 115 tons suitable for the West Indies trade. It stated that anyone interested in purchasing the ship was to contact John Whiddon. He was involved in shipbuilding, carrying on the tradition of his father.

In the early 1770s a petition was submitted to the Honorable William Nelson Esquire, President and Commander in Chief of the Colony of Virginia to protect land in Princess Anne County from being patented. The land included several thousand acres surrounding Cape Henry and was covered with sand dunes and scrub brush. It was unfit for cultivation and was known as the Desert. It served as a common fishing area for the inhabitants of the county and others. The petitioners asked that no patent be granted and that the area be held in common for fishing and other public uses. John Whiddon was a signer of this petition. The land remained a common area for nearly a century before a patent was granted.

John Whiddon and Anne Newton, sister of John's first wife, Elizabeth, inherited property from Captain John Nicholas. This property was located in Newtown, part of Princess Anne County. They sold it in 1777 for 200 pounds.

John owned land in Norfolk and Princess Anne Counties. His holdings were primarily in Norfolk County, including the Western Branch section. Along with his acreage he also purchased a lot in the town of Portsmouth in 1764, at the corner of Court and London. In 1783 he purchased another lot in Portsmouth, at the corner of Crawford and King Streets.

War with England was declared and preparations for war were required. In 1776 John Whiddon was paid 105 pounds for sundry services that he and his servants provided for mounting cannon and working on fortifications in Portsmouth. During its 1780 session the

General Assembly passed an act authorizing the governor to impress supplies needed by the army, with payment to be made at a later time. In 1782 John Whiddon received payment for beef supplied to the army.

On 12 July 1780 the ship *Fanny* sailed from Portsmouth, Virginia headed to St. Eustatius in the Caribbean. She carried a cargo of tobacco. The same day, off the Virginia capes, she was chased and captured by two English warships. A vessel of 30 tons, the *Fanny* had been built earlier that year in Norfolk County. The ship and cargo were owned by John Whiddon, William Skinner and Thomas Mathews. The *Fanny* was lost, a casualty of war.

After a long and prosperous life John Whiddon died 14 April 1796 and was buried in Massenburg Cemetery in Norfolk County. He was the last Whiddon male of this line, as his son, John V, died during the Revolutionary War. This Whiddon line all spent their lives in Norfolk County, Virginia. John left the following will:

> *In the name of God Amen I John Whiddon of Norfolk County Virginia being of sound mind and memory praised be to God for it and knowing that it is appointed all men once to die make and ordain this my Last Will and Testament in manner and form as followeth. First I bequeath my soul to Almighty God who gave it trusting in the merit of the Lord Jesus Christ and my body to the earth to be buried in a decent manner as my Executor and Executrix hereafter shall think fit and all my worldly Estate as well real as personal after all my just debts are paid I give and bequeath in manner and form followeth that is to say:*

> *ITEM I give and bequeath unto my daughter Elizabeth Cunningham, One negro woman called Lettice and her increase to her and her heirs forever. Likewise a piece of land called Rowgally Point containing of fifty eight acres and a half more or less, the place where Samuel Smith formerly lived I give unto her and her heirs for ever. I give and bequeath unto my daughter Mary Broadie a lott of land I purchased of John Archy lying in Portsmouth with all of the improvements on it to her and her heirs forever likewise a piece of land I purchased of George Herbert called Bay*

Tree Hole seventy five acres more or less binding on Davis Ballentine deceased and on my old plantation which land I gave unto her and her heirs forever.

ITEM I give and bequeath unto my daughter Martha Massenburg my old Plantation being the land my father gave me by will likewise fourteen acres of land called Pedley's likewise two acres of land adjoining about three acres more or less called Cartrites Landing being part of the land I purchased of Samuel Smith likewise the land I purchased of Daniel Rhods likewise fifty acres of land I purchased of Samuel Walles called Frissels which land I give unto her and her heirs forever.

ITEM I give and bequeath unto my daughter Ann Peters the plantation where I now live excepting the place called Rowgally Point which I have before willed to my daughter Elizabeth Cunningham and reserving my beloved wife Mary Whiddons life on it then to go to my daughter Ann Peters her and her heirs forever.

ITEM I give and bequeath unto my beloved wife Mary Whiddon the use and property of the whole of the land that I heretofore willed to my daughter Ann Peters during my beloved wifes natural life and the use of all the buildings thereon and the windmill and after my beloved wifes death to fall to my daughter Ann Peters and her heirs forever.

ITEM my will and desire is that the land I purchased of John Cawson adjoining to Samuel Barringon and also the land I purchased of Isaac Edmond likewise the land that came by will of John Nicholas to his daughters Elizabeth and Ann to be sold and the money to be equally divided between my dear beloved wife Mary Whiddon and my four daughters vi; Elizabeth, Mary Martha and Ann.

ITEM I give unto my daughter Martha Massenburg and my daughter Ann Peters each of them ninety pounds current money of Virginia to be paid by my Executrix

ITEM It is my will and desire that my four negro men viz, Sesar, America, Charles and Norfolk George should be hired out yearly and the money arising to go to my loving wife Mary Whiddon for her to dispose of it as She may think proper.

ITEM I give unto my dear beloved wife Mary Whiddon thirteen negroes, viz Andrew, Rose, Lemon, Chaney, Sarah, Jonas, Tom, Priscilla, Sally, Leak, Isaac Boy, Marica, and Mary to her during her natural life likewise all my household furniture and all my Stock, Cattle, Horses, Sheep Hogs... and all my tools and plantation utensils of all kinds during her natural life and after the death of My dear beloved wife Mary Whiddon then it to be equally divided among my four daughters viz; Elizabeth, Mary Martha and Ann.

ITEM lastly for the performance of this my Last Will and Testament I hereby nominate and so appoint my loving wife Mary Whiddon my whole and sole executrix and executor of this my Last Will and Testament revoking all other wills heretofore made in Witness whereof I have hereunto set my hand and seal this twelfth day of April In the year of our Lord one thousand seven hundred and ninety six.

Signed Sealed and acknowledged   John Whiddon – (LS)
To be my last will and testament
In the presence of us, Thomas Tatum,
*   Ann Herbert,*
*   Mayson Ballentine*

The *Norfolk Herald* newspaper of 11 October 1803 discussed placement of a proposed railroad bridge over the Southern Branch of the Elizabeth River. A petition to the General Assembly recommended that the bridge be placed between the shipyard in Portsmouth and Whiddon's Point. Though Whiddon's Point cannot be located today, John Whiddon was prominent enough that even after death, this geographic feature carried his name.

The 1799 Norfolk County tax list shows Mary Whiddon with one of the highest tax assessments in the county. This demonstrates that John left her financially well off. The 1810 census shows Mary in St. Bride's Parish with a number of family living with her. Those living with her may have been a widowed daughter and her children. The tax list also shows Mary with 20 slaves.

Mary Whiddon died 12 January 1818. She was the last to carry the Whiddon name in Norfolk County. She was buried in Massenburg Cemetery with her husband.

John V

John Whiddon, great-great-grandson of the Immigrant, was born about 1753 in Norfolk County, Virginia. He married Ann Herbert on 22 September 1772. They had one daughter, Susannah, who died in 1776 at 18 months old. Susannah was buried in Massenburg Cemetery.

John died during the Revolutionary War. Nothing is known concerning his death, but it is highly probable that he died while serving in the Virginia State Navy. He was born into a seafaring family and many of the Whiddon's family and friends served. Among families that served in Virginia's Navy were the Herberts, Cunninghams, Markhams and Nicholas, all closely associated with the Whiddon family.

During the Revolution, America was unable to protect its coasts due to the lack of a federal navy. To combat the powerful English Navy, each state began to provide its own navy. Virginia established one of the strongest navies of any state. More than 80 vessels served in the Virginia State Navy. In December of 1775, the Virginia Convention resolved:

> *And for the greater security of the inhabitants of this colony from depredations of the enemy by water be it ordained that the committee of safety shall and they are hereby empowered and required to provide from time to time such and so many armed vessels as they may judge necessary for the protection of the several rivers in this colony, in the best manner the circumstances of the country will permit: and to that end, to raise and take into pay a sufficient number of officers and men, as well sailors and marines...*

Severely overmatched by the English Navy, most of Virginia's vessels were either captured or destroyed. Virginia sailors, who survived an encounter with the enemy, were taken prisoner. Many were placed on

English prison ships. Conditions onboard these vessels were horrible and many American sailors died during captivity. Few records remain to identify these American prisoners.

John's widow, Ann, married Thomas Herbert on 4 July 1778. Thomas was the son of Captain Markham Herbert and Mary Whiddon, daughter of Captain John Whiddon.

Line of Descent of Augustine, Son of the Immigrant

Augustine

Augustine Whiddon, youngest son of the Immigrant, was born about 1662 in Lower Norfolk County, Virginia. He was called a carpenter in his will. He may have been involved in shipbuilding, as was much of the Whiddon family.

Augustine appears on certificates of importation for his brother John in 1678 and for his brother William in 1690.

Augustine married Sarah Cherry, daughter of John and Elizabeth Faithful Cherry, and they had three sons, John, Augustine and William.

In 1684 Augustine Whiddon purchased 200 acres on Deep Creek from Matthew Caswell. The land is mentioned in Augustine's will. Later, Caswell was again in possession of this property. Whether Caswell reclaimed the property due to failure of Augustine to fully pay for it or he bought it back is not known.

The sons of Augustine were minors at the writing of his will in 1690. The will was proved in 1693 and is as follows:

> In the name of God Amen, I Augustine Whiddon, of the County of Lower Norfolk Carpenter being perfect in sense and memory Blessed God the Almighty, and although sick and weak in body therefore doe ordain this my Last Will and Testament, Imprimis, I doe bequeath my soul to the Almighty God that gave it and my body to the earth to be decently buried in hope of a glorious resurrection, and as for

*my temporal estate I doe bequeath as followeth to my loving
wife Sarah Whiddon during her natural life, and like wise I
doe give her all my houses and plantation I now live on for
her during her natural life, and likewise I doe give her all
my personal estate…and as for the land I doe give my son
John Whiddon after the death of my wife, the plantation
including one hundred acres of land now adjoining to it, and
the other hundred to be equally divided between my other
sons Augustine and William to them aforesaid and their
heirs forever, but provided John dyes in his minority, then the
house and his hundred acres to fall to Augustine, William
to have the other hundred, and if one of the youngest dye the
other the younger brother to have his fifty acres and I doe will
that all three of my sons shall be free of age at eighteen years
of age. It is to be understood that my eldest son John shall
have only the hundred acres aforesaid and if my wife dyes,
I doe give the children unto my father in law, John Cherry
and to his wife, and I do make and appoint my loving wife
Sarah Executrix of this my Last Will and Testament as
written by my hand this 13th of September 1690.*

Written & delivered	*Proved by the oaths*
in the presence of us	*Wm. Maunde & John Cherry Sen.*
William Maunde	*this 16th of May 1693*
John Cherry Sr.	
Thomas Biggs	

Sarah made a Deed of Gift at the time Augustine's will was proved.
The Deed of Gift to her sons is as follows:

*Know all men by these present that I, Sarah Whiddon of
the Southern Branch of the Elizabeth River widdow; for and
in consideration of the true love and affection that I have for
my children doe by virtue of this Deed of Gift give them
as followeth to be delivered when they come to age, Imp:
to my son John one gunn and one fower gallon pott, one
box about fower foote long and one heifer that was bought
of Isaac Seaborne, with this exception, the first cowe calf to*

Augustine that shee brings, the next to William both which of my sons to have the female increase if any, and two sows and piggs, to be delivered to my son John Whiddon that year that he is of age, and I doe give my son Augustine, one gunn and one pott of a gallon and a halfe, and one box three foote long, and one bed and boster and one pair of blankets, and bedstead, and two sowes and pigs, if either of them dyes before they come to age, his share to be equally divided to the others, In witness to the foresaid present, I have sett my hand this 12th of May 1693.

Signed and Delivered in presence of   Sarah Whiddon
Wm. Maunde   her mark
Acknowledged in Court 16 May 1693

After Augustine's death, Sarah married Thomas Willson. He died in 1702, and she married again to Eleazar Tart in 1705.

The orphaned sons of Augustine disappeared into the mist of history. No evidence concerning them has been found. They may have changed their last name, all died or moved from the area. This ended the short line of Augustine Whiddon.

Concluding Thoughts

Every family has an interesting and important story to tell and certainly the Whiddon family is no exception. Our story is interesting because it helps us connect with a proud past and is important because it helps us understand how we influence the future.

The experience of discovering my heritage has given me a feeling of familiarity with many of the people about whom I have written. Genealogical research is like a telescope into the past that tells us much about our ancestors, but from a distance. I feel like I know much about them but I have many questions I would like to ask. Primarily, I wonder what they would think of the legacy they wrought.

This book is dedicated to my grandchildren; they are too young to enjoy learning about their heritage but hopefully in time they will appreciate this journey of discovery. In the mean time, others are welcome to take the journey with me.

I have diligently tried to correct errors found in previous works. I hope the future produces researchers who will expand on and correct errors in my work.

"Those who do not look upon themselves as a link connecting the past with the future do not perform their duty to the world"

Daniel Webster

Primary Sources

Allen County Public Library Foundation (PERSI)
Chesapeake Public Library, Wallace Memorial Room
Clerk's Office, Circuit Court of the City of Chesapeake
Darlington County Historical Commission, Darlington, SC
Decatur County Courthouse, Bainbridge, GA
Genealogical Center Library, Marietta, GA
Georgia State Archives
National Archives and Records Administration
Norfolk Public Library, Sargeant Memorial Room
North Carolina State Archives
Old Darlington District Chapter, S. C. G. S., Hartsville, SC
Outer Banks History Center, Manteo, NC
Portsmouth Public Library, Virginia History Room
South Carolina Department of Archives & History
The Library of Virginia
The Mariners' Museum Library, Newport News, VA
UK National Archives
Westcountry Studies Library, Exeter, Devon, UK

www.ingramcontent.com/pod-product-compliance
Lightning Source LLC
Chambersburg PA
CBHW020311290526
45784CB00003B/1474

* 9 7 8 1 4 3 8 9 2 9 8 4 2 *